PSYCHOTHERAPY: A CHRISTIAN APPROACH

By E. N. DUCKER

A Christian Therapy for a Neurotic World

PSYCHOTHERAPY
A Christian Approach

BY

E. N. DUCKER

FOREWORD BY DR E. GRAHAM HOWE

London
GEORGE ALLEN & UNWIN LTD
RUSKIN HOUSE MUSEUM STREET

PRINTED IN GREAT BRITAIN
BY WILLMER BROTHERS AND HARAM LTD
BIRKENHEAD

To
The Right Reverend The Lord
Bishop of Leicester
by whose permission this
work has continued

Again, the devil taketh him up into an exceeding high mountain, and sheweth him all the kingdoms of the world, and the glory of them; and saith unto him, all these things will I give thee, if thou wilt fall down and worship me. Then saith Jesus unto him. Get thee hence, Satan: for it is written, Thou shalt worship the Lord thy God, and him only shalt thou serve.

St Matthew, IV, 8–10.

The fact that the mind rules the body is, in spite of its neglect by biology and medicine, the most fundamental fact we know about the process of life.

FRANZ ALEXANDER—
Psychosomatic Medicine.

. . . the wholeness of Christ's way of life was the personal relationship between the believer and the Lord, the freedom and spontaneity and adventurousness of discipleship, and the reliance not upon external precept but upon inward constraint. The difference (between New Testament and Catholic Christendom) was that between a walk along a strictly fenced path where every stage is marked and no wayfarer can go astray, and an expedition over unmapped country and a companion who knows the lie of the land—the one as dull as a treadmill, and the other a voyage of discovery.

C. E. RAVEN—
*Natural Religion and
Christian Theology*, vol. 11.

FOREWORD

Whether we choose to believe it or not, life is in fact for all of us, but for some much more than others, a very frightening experience. From the point of vantage of our security, it is only right and reasonable, as it is also instinctively natural, for us to escape from danger if we can, to some better place with safety. As psychologists, parsons, teachers or any of us who occupy positions of privilege as leaders in our society, there are many ways of sitting safely on a shelf, as critics and advisers rather than as participants in the battle of life.

To all of us who have perhaps thus been more successful in our escape from the full experiences of life's distress, will come from time to time those who have been less successful, who have in fact fallen between the two alternatives of TRUTH on the one hand, and escape into phantasy on the other. Perhaps such people may have been too tied to their innermost TRUTH, ever to have become entirely disloyal to it? In spite of centuries of brainwashing and years of parental misleading and misunderstanding, for some are too sincere to lose the gift of it, the TRUTH remains, to drive them either into sickness or delinquency, as their only refuge from the 'double-bind' in which, whatever 'I' may do, 'I' must always be wrong.

So what shall we, who have been more successful than they, do for those who have only come to terms with life by becoming sad or sick, the sorry, or not-so-sorry, problems of society?

As parsons or psychologists, teachers or magistrates, we find ourselves in a position of *power over* such people. We can advise or instruct, condemn or punish them. As their 'superiors' we can, and usually do, mistreat them as our 'inferiors', in order to preserve our personal status of one-up-manship, securely unimpaired.

But Christ, who may seem to be strange company for modern psychotherapists, declared and behaved otherwise. 'Love your enemies,' he said.

Although psychologists are as various as Christians in their opinions, they are agreed in one matter: which is, that the problem of any 'one' is to relate himself to his 'duality', by living through the stress of this relationship with his alien, unfriendly and apparently destructive, 'other'. If I can live with my other self, I can more easily bear to live with you. But if I hate myself, I shall certainly hate you. As Shakespeare said: 'Love, loving not itself, none other can.' From this derives the practise of all effective psychotherapy. However diverse the worlds of psychology and theology may seem to be, they can still learn to live together, and learn from one another, as long as they do not assume too much similarity, or fear too much difference.

One advantage possessed by Christians is that they know and practise what they know; which is that of ourselves we have no power over the other, not even healing power. All power is THINE, not MINE. Psychologists suffer from lack of this certainty. Believing that they have no power in themselves to heal, they therefore remain somewhat negatively bewildered as to whence this grace is given, and may find themselves under pressure to offer alternative rational explanations, where none is really required.

Canon Ducker is not in any sense fanatically 'sold' to psychology. He remains throughout critically detached, preferring to read from the truth revealed to him by his patient's experiences and dreams, rather than from any of the psychological text books. His experience of life illuminates what he reads, whether of psychology or the Gospels. He seems to draw even his religion, and certainly his psychology, from his reading of the pages of experience.

He sees the future as a threat, which indeed it has always been. He asked the question, whose Ark will ride the coming flood? He sees the need for training and more training, for any who hope to heal the sick and make the partial whole. But meanwhile, he sees the need for living dangerously and suffering enough damage to our egoic defences, if ever we are to allow the TRUTH to set us free.

Canon Ducker makes plain that there is sufficient common ground between psychologists and clergy, as between 'our selves' and 'the others', for us to be able to live and work together. If, as I believe, our differences derive largely from our misunderstanding of one another, this book will do much useful work by diminishing misunderstanding, and so adding to our effectiveness as healers amongst the many ills of our disordered world.

E. GRAHAM HOWE
37 Queen Anne Street,
London W.1

PREFACE

Since writing A *Christian Therapy for a Neurotic World* I have been asked by several doctors, amongst other people, when I should be contributing another volume. Owing to considerable pressure of work, this seemed a remote possibility. However, I was invited to give the 1962 Lent Lectures in the Cathedral by the Provost and Chapter of Leicester. It is difficult to say 'No' to friends, and because I feel that my diocese, to which I have been attached for a quarter of a century, has been kind to me in various ways, I could do no other than accept their kind invitation. These lectures form the basis of a large part of this book, and I am grateful to the Provost for his ready consent to my using them in this way. They have been extended and re-shaped. Further, a paper written on Psychosomatic Medicine and read to the hospital Chaplains of Derbyshire has been incorporated, along with other relevant material. Chapter 10 was added later.

The aim of this book is the same as that of its predecessor, to present the comparatively new science of Psychology as a handmaid of Religion. It is also an attempt to convince many doubting Thomases, which is a very difficult task, for plain words cannot express the dreadful emotional pain and the paralysing effects of unconscious fantasy which so many minds endure. Pictures come the nearest to making something of this suffering known, but these unfortunately are very costly to reproduce. A Harley Street acquaintance of mine, a man of very wide reputation and the author of many notable works on psychotherapy, gave up writing books because he came to realize the impossibility of communication by word of the depths of human experience. In a similar way religious experience baffles description, and any attempt to express it appears either trite or extravagant. In spite of all the difficulties I have written this book in a further attempt to convince the doubters, and to this end I have drawn heavily upon my patients who generously allow their material to be used in this way. Further, I have written it as simply as I possibly can, avoiding excursions into psychological theory.

For twelve years now a major part of my ministry has been devoted to this specialist service as part of the Ministry of the Church. The results have been abundantly rewarding both in regard to the help given to people in desperate need, and to the strengthening of the Church. I can appreciate that the novelty of this approach, with its new concepts and terminology, is found difficult for some people to grasp, and for others it is frightening. But neither of these reasons absolves us from the duty of persevering with this ministry, for, as Jacob found, such wrestling leaves a blessing behind.

13

The encouragement received over the publication of my former book, apart from that given by the Bishop of Leicester, came chiefly from the medical profession, but also from many ordinary readers. I hope this volume will be found helpful, and that it will be taken by some of them as a substitute for personal appearances. Every day brings evidence of the great interest there is in the subject, and I could easily spend the whole of my time addressing meetings of one kind or another. Because I put my patients before all diversions I have to ration myself very severely with regard to the time I give to this kind of thing, otherwise my patients would suffer, and their resentment would retard their progress. Only by writing can I pass on my experience in this ministry, and this has to be done in the very early hours of the morning.

A question has been raised as to whether the cases in my books are selected on account of their very special and exceptional interest, and that in fact most cases which come for treatment are somewhat humdrum. Naturally some disorders are more complex than others, but when dealing with any disorder of a serious kind, such as are the majority of those presented to me for treatment, the details will always be of special interest. Any case of serious disorder will not be adequately treated unless it is pursued in depth to the complex infantile situation. Tinkering about on the surface may produce some benefit, probably of a temporary nature, but nothing short of a radical cure should be our aim, and in such cases, one might say without exception, case material of considerable interest will be presented.

For a more detailed account of this work and for further reading on the subject I would refer readers to the bibliography in my *Christian Therapy for a Neurotic World* (Allen & Unwin). However, I must mention three recent books, two by R. D. Laing, *The Divided Self*, and *The Self and Others* (Tavistock), which are not easy books and they are not for the beginner. Another book is small and readable, and it is most valuable; it is Anthony Storr's *The Integrity of the Personality* (Heinemann).

I wish to thank my good friends again for their help: my teacher the Reverend E. W. P. Ingham, Dr G. D. Yeoman, the Reverend Peter Etchells for his meticulous care in reading the proof and for compiling an index, and to my son John for valuable help in various ways. Finally, I am indebted to Dr E. Graham Howe who generously contributed the Foreword and thereby has given encouragement which is greatly valued.

1962

CONTENTS

ACKNOWLEDGEMENTS

Acknowledgement is made to the following publishers from whose books short quotations have been made: George Allen & Unwin *Psychosomatic Medicine* by Dr Alexander; Gerald Duckworth *Emotional Conflict* by Peter Fletcher; Hodder & Stoughton *The Unutterable Beauty* by Studdert-Kennedy; Routledge & Kegan Paul *The Psychogenesis of Mental Disease* by C. G. Jung, *Memories, Dreams, Reflections* by C. G. Jung, *Conditions of Nervous Anxiety* by W. Stekel; Cambridge University Press *Natural Religion and Christian Theology* by C. E. Raven.

CHAPTER 1

IT IS DANGEROUS!

Dangerous situations call for dangerous action, not retreat. There is no need to catalogue the dangers which confront the Church in our day. In some way or other there have always been dangers, and always will be, but this is no excuse for not dealing with the difficulties before us. We must do what we can whilst there is time, remembering that opportunities can be lost. Church history has been strewn with lost opportunities like the stars in number, and this is no matter for complaisance. C. G. Jung demonstrated how that all life is lived in a state of tension between the pull of opposites, and it is clear that the Church is set between a daring spirit of adventure and the deadly attractiveness of safety-first, between progression and regression, the ancient and the modern. Religion can be the most alive thing or it can be the most death-like. 'Can these bones live?' was first asked by Ezekiel and many others have since asked this question. It is possible to transform those dead bones into a mighty living army, and we should always be alive to the present deadness within us and the possibility of new life. However, it is dangerous to have close dealings with the dead for, by their contamination, they may pull us down into the pit. Further, some people prefer to be dead, and they make an excellent case for this peaceful state.

> This day I set before you both life and death, the blessing and the cursing.   (*Deuteronomy* XXX, 19.)

This book is concerned with the application of scientific psychology to the understanding of man from the Christian point of view. The earlier volume A *Christian Therapy for a Neurotic World* dealt with this unification in some detail, and it demonstrated how the life of the Church is in fact enriched by this pursuit. It is a new field, just as psychology is a new science; and it deals with what is essentially the concern of religion, the soul of man. Its province is what man is within himself and man's relatedness to other persons, which are inseparable.

It is to be doubted that there is anywhere more misunderstanding and sheer prejudice than there is regarding psychology. People defend themselves against it by cracking jokes about it, or they sneer at it by treating it as airy-fairy theorizing. The most common defence against it is to say it is dangerous, which is intended to banish it to the ends of the earth. There is a universal fear of psychology. It is regarded as dangerous because it confronts us with the unknown, it delves deeply into the unconscious which is undoubtedly frightening to us all because it contains the most primitive part of life and our own hidden personal past. We are naturally afraid of that which we cannot control by conscious thought, and madness is regarded to be just that. But if we think about it we shall soon see that there is much of ourselves, and perhaps the most valuable part of ourselves, which is irrational, for our feelings carry us into the heights and depths of experience. Nevertheless, people widely think that rational control is the one sure criterion of sanity, and therefore to pass out of this realm of light into the darkness of our underworld, or overworld as it may be, is a sure way to ask for trouble. 'It is dangerous to meddle—Danger, keep out.'

There is no need for this fear, for there are many levels in our deep mind and only in the case of serious emotional sickness is it necessary to go down into these depths. The cure of many of the common emotional disorders need take us only to the highest layers of the unconscious of which no one should be afraid. After all, we all are more or less neurotic, and no one should feel he is odd when he feels out of sorts with himself and other people. Indeed it is just our own oddness which makes us interesting. Just imagine everyone being wholly cured of these oddities and being made completely balanced, and you will see a world of the dullest people possible. Everyone would be more or less the same and that would be truly appalling. Therapy should make a person more of an individual and at the same time a citizen with a richer contribution to make to the life of the whole.

If we are by nature afraid of our unconscious it is altogether another thing to deem psychology dangerous because it shatters the fantasies we delight in. It is dangerous to all forms of pretence and self-deception. It shatters every form of evasion of the truth. There are many false fronts which we wear in order to impress our neighbours, and the insidious thing about this deception is that we are unaware that we are doing it. The person most of all deceived is himself. No wonder, then, that we see this instrument of self-revelation as dangerous! The castles and ivory towers we build are for ever shattered and we find ourselves amongst the ruins having to build a genuine life from the beginning. The mighty fallen need all the courage and faith conceivable to set about this task. But what does it matter so long as truth and reality are the gain, for to build on any other foundation is to build upon sand, or to build something which can never be completed. 'Ye shall know the truth,' said Jesus, 'and the truth shall make you free.'

I have seen this happen more times than I can remember. I have seen people stripped of their defences because of their unreality, and I have witnessed the decline and fall of spiritual empires only to be replaced by renewed spiritual vigour and a living religion. In every department of life the right thing can be done for the wrong motive. A man in his forties produced this dream: 'I was in church, and it was Mass. The Vicar was there swinging a thurible, and I noticed through the cloud of incense that the Vicar was smoking a cigarette. He then called to three women dressed in red (scarlet women). These went round the church sprinkling the congregation with corn flakes.' This dream was the last of a trilogy. In the first he had dealt with his falsity regarding his attitudes towards his father, in the second he did likewise regarding his mother, and finally here he is exposing his false attitudes in his religion. He was debunking his spiritual unreality. He had been hiding behind a smoke screen which was his religion. He still goes to his church but differently, and his church life is no longer a game to be played with his sick conscience, but his religion has become real. He could easily have said 'This psychology is dangerous, it upsets one's values and life-long usages.' Had he done so he would still have been deceiving himself and others.

The average person in this modern world is generally sceptical and even afraid of the operations of the Holy Spirit. Not only is it true of the present day, but also of times past. Like the wind, there is no telling 'whence it cometh or whither it goeth.' (St John III–8.)

To live by the Spirit is therefore to live by faith, relying on something that is by its very nature intangible and indefinite. For who knows into what dangers it might lead us, or what next of our cherished positions in life might be dynamited by it?

People whose lives are basically insecure naturally tend to that which brings them security. They hold fast to tradition, the unchanging social customs and that which is familiar to them and therefore 'safe' to live and deal with. Like the priest and the Levite in the parable (St Luke X–30ff.) they will seek to save their skins whenever a challenging or disturbing situation arises. It would appear to them that their proudest and most jealously guarded possession, status, is threatened by the Spirit, the 'unknowable factor'. To defend themselves against the dangers of such threats, they proceed to build a wall within themselves that will stand solidly against all their fears of insecurity.

Such people tend to exaggerate the importance of the rational facets of life to the utmost giving no ground to the spiritual undertones which are vital to 'wholeness'. Fixed patterns of belief and practice are then imposed upon themselves, affecting not only their own outlook, but also the outlook of those around them. They impose upon others their own self-made responsibilities and safety precautions. The status quo soon becomes a matter of life and death, they feel they must preserve the old wine-skins at all costs (St Matthew IX–17).

Their religion is also caught up in this moulding process. It becomes a suit off the peg rather than a suit that fully fits the wearer. This religious 'suit' must be made to fit somehow, but to be fully comprehended, religion must be hammered to size by the individual on the anvil of his own particular life; it must be a personal discovery within the human situation.

In saying all this, I am not trying to belittle the traditions of either past or present, far from it. What I am trying to say is that tradition has very little value of itself. To be of value, it must be fitted into the drama of our personal existence and related to the problems of modern living. Unless this can be understood, the personality stands to suffer a grievous loss and much sickness. The Bible is repeatedly brought to light by the unconscious minds of patients undergoing analysis; through it, the blind have their eyes opened and the deaf hear. Ancient doctrines then, and only then, become real to them.

Before this awakening can take place, there must be a prolonged wandering in the wilderness on the part of the patient searching for his goal, and the smiting of many a hard rock, which no one would choose to do save in dire necessity. In other words, the basis of religion is sacrifice. We must learn to relax the Egyptian security that surrounds us all, we must stand to lose all we have in order to gain the immeasurably great reward of Life.

In the aforementioned parable, the priest and the Levite represent this same fear-ridden security. But both had anaesthetized themselves against this fear. Their anaesthetic was tradition, and their well-built castles of 'piety'. Jesus was crucified for the same reason, that He had become a threat to such defences and had opened their eyes to the deepest fears of life. On the other hand, the Good Samaritan had no defensive position to maintain, and therefore was free to run risks. In this respect he was empty, holding on to nothing that would prevent his freedom and fulfilment.

The concern for self-maintenance is a great enemy of life, just as sacrifice is the means whereby life is possessed. Psychotherapy is based on one's readiness to 'burn one's boats', a great leap of faith indeed: perhaps this is why it has so many critics, as this rewarding venture would appear to be a most fearful and dangerous thing.

Psychology is dangerous to our tranquillity. Who likes to be dis-

turbed? We are devoted slaves to routine and the conventional because these things carry us along without thought and effort. The
very mention of the word tradition may send a warm glow through
our being. It speaks of security and well worn paths along which it
is safe to travel, it is the guarantee of clearly defined landmarks. We
need in truth all the help the past can bring to us, but to live wholly
in the past, if apparently safe, is wholly inadequate in each new age.
This unwillingness to be disturbed was the daily burden of the
prophets who were asked not to speak the truth:

'this is a rebellious people, lying children, children that will not hear
the Law of the Lord: which say to the seers, See not; and to the
prophets, Prophesy not unto us right things, speak unto us smooth
things, prophesy deceits . . .'   (Isaiah XXX-9, 10.)

Psychology is dangerous to our conceit. It is humiliating to find we
are not the God-like creatures we imagined ourselves to be. How many
of our motives will stand the test of psychological insight? Confession
in the ecclesiastical sense is beneficial, but its scope is seen as superficial when compared with the searching light of analysis where
'there is nothing hid that shall not be revealed.' Of course, the
majority of people are not required to undergo such drastic treatment,
and Confession may well be adequate. Yet how much more effective
the Church's counsels would be were they informed by the new insights into human motives, and by an ability to distinguish between
sin and moral disease.[1] No one undergoes an analysis without considerable suffering, for it is shocking and devastating to come face to
face with the truth about ourselves in this way. Something of this
shock therapy would be added to the Church's ministry were the
majority of the clergy aware of the help which psychology can give.
The life of the Church would be transformed in this way, the clergy
first taking a new look at themselves. We might not like it, but there
is no question as to the great benefits to be derived therefrom. Pride
would be hurt as it was by our Lord's penetrating insight into the
inner life of the Pharisee and Sadducee. The scales from many eyes
would have to fall, and the new light would at first be blinding, for
those who have long lived in the darkness are pained by the light.

It is said that it is dangerous to dabble in psychology. I could not
agree more. I have written previously about the need to be adequately
trained to deal in depth psychotherapy. 'Counselling' is excellent, and
it requires not a little psychological knowledge. This is altogether
different from a full therapeutic ministry for which specialized train-

[1] Cf. A. J. Hadfield—*Psychology and Morals*, pp. 56, 57.

ing is required. I hope the day will not be far distant when the Church trains a selected few persons, clerical or lay, for this work. I am convinced that 'Counselling' needs deep psychotherapy to come to its help in the more difficult cases. It is one thing to dabble in psychology, but it is a totally different thing to practise it after specialized training.

Of course, there are definite dangers, but it is just these that training overcomes. People can be treated who should not be given an analysis. Sometimes it is not possible to discern their full condition at first, and no one is to blame should it turn out to be so. The therapist will be able to read the signs, the writing on the wall, and take other steps. This therapy is altogether different from other branches of medicine, for in this case completely correct treatment may be given and the patient may worsen. It is not the fault of the therapist, and perhaps not of the patient, for he may lack the courage to face the issue. And no one can say beforehand how the person will react when the vital point is reached. Thus in serious cases there is always some risk, and therefore danger. Fortunately the number of people who run away are a small minority.

It may be said that it is dangerous to obtrude into a sphere which belongs to another profession. Emotional sickness is sometimes said to be the prerogative of the medical profession. This we emphatically deny. The Church has always practised Clinical Theology and she should never have allowed herself to be edged out of the realm of the soul's therapy. If religion is not concerned with the inner life of man what nonsense is made of religion! Psychology is deeply concerned with love and relatedness. These are the core of psychology, and this is just what religion is about.

'Thou shalt love the Lord thy God . . .
and thy neighbour as thyself.'

I do not think it is at all realized that the therapy here envisaged is almost only obtainable at very considerable cost from a handful of doctors in Harley Street. The National Health Service does not provide for such treatment. The help given at our mental hospitals is of a different kind, and we leave such treatments as they give in their hands. But there is something different we offer through an alliance with psychotherapy, and this is pre-eminently our sphere, and we are failing by not operating in it.

Some people may be fearful that we are attempting to set up the Church in opposition to the medical profession. I hasten to say that there are times when the two spheres of activity are entirely distinct, but there are other times when the two overlap, and this in a crucial regard. In this latter case it is patently wrong for the Church, through ignorance or lack of courage, to contract out of her responsibility, and hand over the sick person 'in toto' to the doctor. My own experience has shown me again and again that, when the confidence of the doctor has been gained, he is only too ready to accept all the help the Church can give towards the recovery of his patient. The doctor who has the welfare of his patient at heart wants above all else to see him made well again, by any means and regardless of his professional pride. Of course, there are doctors who have no room in their science and philosophy for anything savouring of the spiritual, and by this many of them would include psychology. When the Church speaks officially of co-operation with the doctors she is inclined only to envisage extraneous comforts and consolations rather than a radical coping with the illness; she may hope for a miracle rather than use insights, within her sphere, in the service of her Lord. To the faint-hearted and the dubious, and even to the fearful, I would say it is dangerous not to use this new instrument, for by neglect other people will come and use it in a materialistic way, and the Church will remain a voice crying in the wilderness with not an ear to hear.

This is borne out by the fact that more and more people are turning to the doctor rather than to the clergyman for advice and help with their personal problems. It would never cross their minds for a moment that the parson is the person to whom they should go for this kind of help. This attitude may have been born out of long experience of clergy whose function appears to be wholly irrelevant to the real problems of life. Perhaps it is also that they think the solid pills of the doctor are more efficacious than piety, and that the doctor's unconcern with the growth and healing of the soul is more realistic. They would rather have the doctor's kind of 'salvation' than that of the parson. But this medical kind of salvation, which is pre-occupied with the preservation of the 'status quo', is, in many a case, completely inadequate, and with this many a Christian doctor would heartily agree. The fact remains that to many people the Church's kind of salvation somehow misses the point when it comes to dealing with human problems, especially with those the roots of which lie deeply embedded in the unconscious. A change of attitude can only be brought about when people discover that the Church can help in a new and vital way. Believe me, there is an opportunity wide open not only to help the people without her borders but also to renew the vigour and sincerity of those who stand within her gates. Here is a new field for faith and that venturous spirit which, in many ages past, has been the singular glory of the Church of Jesus Christ.

There is another reason why it is dangerous for the Church to neglect the findings of analytical psychology. It would appear that within the next fifty years there will take place a revolution in human thought equal to that any man has ever known, the repercussions of which will test the foundations of preconceived thought. Startling discoveries have already been made known in the realm of genetics, but these promise to be but the first rumblings of a tremendous and frightening storm. Vast sums of money are being spent upon research in this direction, particularly by Russia, which country is wholly out of sympathy with personalistic psychology. It concerns the *physical* basis of psychology and indeed of all values. We need to prepare for this revolution by becoming thoroughly conversant with the emotional processes which lie at the root of personality, and the effects of emotions upon the physical processes of the body. The Church cannot afford to lose any time at all in becoming fully aware of the reality of the emotional causation within the personality. The immaterial and spiritual dimensions will then be in a far better position to hold their ground, backed by experience. It is dangerous not to do this.

NOTE ON THE RELATIONSHIP BETWEEN CONFESSOR AND ANALYST

Reference having been made to Confession something further needs to be said about so important a function of the Church. The role of the analyst can easily be confused with that of the confessor. Fr Victor White O.P. in the chapter on 'The Analyst and the Confessor' in his book *God and the Unconscious* examines the two functions, and although he shows how they can be mistakenly identified, he argues that their mutual acquaintance is most beneficial.

The differences between the analyst and the confessor are that the former pursues an unfettered and unique exploration of an uncharted sea, whereas the latter follows determined and conventional patterns. Again, the one is concerned with the evil men suffer, while the other with the evil they do. As Fr Victor White said, there is all the difference between misfortune and misdeeds; the one deals with compulsions we cannot help, the other with the responsibility of human freedom; the one is blameless, the other blameworthy, which is, of course, speaking as a generalization. Furthermore, one is dealing with the unconscious and the other with the conscious, one with what is, apart from analysis, unknown and unknowable, the other with what is known or knowable. The analyst is not limited to a single life-time, for he has often to deal with what comes down from generations past in the Collective Unconscious, but the confessor is. The former deals with parts of the self which are, in a large measure, beyond control, whereas the confessor works in the realm of the will and responsible behaviour. The attitude of the analyst is completely relaxed, but that of the confessor is one of concentration and discipline. The one only seeks to understand, the other accepts and encourages the acknowledgement of blame, and in so doing the analyst confronts the patient with himself, whilst the confessor brings the penitent face to face with God.

However, if there are so many real differences as these there are also important ways in which the confessor's work draws very close to that of the analyst. He will be a far better confessor if he understands the part that unconscious motivation plays in a person's life; he will be able to see the part the infantile background has played amongst many other things, and his spiritual direction will take in many more factors than it would without this special knowledge. The analyst also will find himself confronted with religious issues in which he feels himself to be out of his depth, and he may be tempted to treat such things as irrelevant to life.

There is, in fact, a common ground upon which both the analyst and the confessor meet, for moral issues are always rising, guilt is always something which has to be dealt with, and conscience, true or false, is involved in most human situations: and sooner or later the analyst will have to make the patient aware of vital choices in life. He will have to help his patient to see that self-pity is barring the way to wholeness, the cries against injustices suffered, and the demands made upon the universe, only turn the patient in upon himself in self-love, make him dependent in a sick way upon others, angry and complaining, unco-operative and greedy, playing-up and evasive. All neurotic disorders have their secret gains and pleasures, which must be uncovered and faced before the patient is set free from his complaint. This is a deep moral issue, and for many people a profoundly religious one. The patient must come to accept the necessity of dying in order to live, and be ready to suffer the pains of re-birth; in fact, he must discover in the depths of his experience the truth of our Lord's words :

'Whosoever shall seek to save his life shall lose it;
and whosoever shall lose his life shall preserve it.'
(St *Luke* XVII, 33.)

CHAPTER 2

SELF-SUFFICIENCY

When we look at people in the street they appear to us to be going about on their lawful occasions without a care in the world. So it seems. But could we read the secrets of their hearts we should find each person, known or unknown to himself, carrying, like Pilgrim, a great burden on his back. These burdens are of such a nature that they impede effective living, drain off our energies into futile channels, sadden our spirits, tire out or make sick our bodies, impair our character and retard spiritual growth. Besides that, these burdens also fall on to others' shoulders, often those we least want to hurt—husband or wife, parents or children. The weight of the burden we carry may at times bring us to a complete standstill, so that we cannot work and we withdraw from essential relationships, or it may consume us with inescapable emotional entanglements. In extreme cases this secret but heavy burden can and does end in suicide.

The Church is failing the Lord of Life grievously if she has nothing to say in such situations. How can she, as a representative of our Lord, repeat 'Come unto me ye burden-bearers, and I will give you rest' unless she has at her disposal the remedy which can bring men to that rest? Alas, there are all too often words in plenty, but of a wrong kind, which may only add 'burdens grievous to be borne.' Through a new understanding of the depths of human experience something more than words is today forthcoming from the Church, and she is becoming engaged with the human situation in a new way, one that removes those life-long burdens, and brings healing to the body, mind and spirit.

I have chosen to tell you about Harry in order to show how hard life can become for some people, and the reactions that are set up in consequence. He is fifty-four years of age. His parents were chronic neurotics. His father was a dipsomaniac, almost always out of work, and frequently he would disappear from home for long periods, whilst his mother had no love for the twelve children she bore. Her irresponsibility matched that of her husband, and Harry described her as 'twitchy and fussy', and as an unlovable character.

He lived his childhood under terrible conditions, in extreme poverty and filth, in a house with only two bedrooms, no lavatory and no water. He said, 'We lived in a block of houses in the . . . area known as "the mud houses". We were filthy, verminous, hungry, ill-clothed, and always lived in terror. It is no wonder we are all neurotics.' He told me that there were two beds in the house, and that he well remembered there being at least six in one bed and of both sexes. He said, 'My mother and father fought and behaved like wild animals, and I shall never forget as long as I live, my father, after one beastly fight with my mother, throwing the baby of the family into the fireplace; luckily the child was rescued by a neighbour. We children used to huddle together during these constant fights, hiding anywhere we could, upstairs, under chairs, outside the house, anywhere, sobbing and screaming all the time.'

'At the age of sixteen,' he continued, 'I ran away from home and joined the armed forces. I lied about my age and was accepted into the Royal Army Medical Corps. In those days of little pay, and even less glamour, in the Army, I was really happy for the first time in my life. I had clothes, food, companions, clean living conditions, and a bed to sleep in with real sheets. It was heaven to me, in spite of the fact that on arrival at the depot, the hairdresser completely shaved my head because it was verminous—the only one among all the recruits.' He could never blot this particular incident out of his mind, and the shame of it, a symbol of all his childhood's shame, subsequently haunted him wherever he went.

His father eventually discovered where he was, and he wrote demanding that Harry paid him five shillings out of his weekly fourteen shillings, otherwise he would inform the authorities that he was under age and take him back home again. Harry said that he would have willingly given his father all his pay just to stay where he was. When he went abroad he paid his father 3s 6d out of his daily 5s 6d, to keep for him pending his return so that he would have enough money to marry. Later a sister informed him that every penny of it had been spent by his parents, mainly by his father. There should have been £250 in savings, no small sum in those days. However, he advanced in his corps, was awarded special promotion, became a qualified trained nurse, a T.A. instructor and dispenser, and was awarded the Leishman Prize for the best papers on dispensing for the year. He also became an educational instructor. In 1936 he was appointed Acting Sergeant Major, and three years later he was commissioned, finally becoming a Major with the award of M.B.E. He was mentioned in despatches, and given the Long Service and Good Conduct Medals. At the end of the war misfortune hit him once again. He was given a permanent commission, and in all probability he would today be holding the rank of Lieutenant-Colonel, with an excellent prospect of good gratuity and pension. This should have followed, but it was as though something within him made him act contrary to himself and his best interests. He resigned his commission, and took various kinds of work in succession, each with its tale of set-back and failure.

When I first saw Harry he made a considerable impression upon me. He was physically strong, and tough, in fact all that one would associate with a professional soldier. There was a twinkle in his eyes, and yet, when off his guard, one could see clear evidence of the inner stress, and the burden on his soul which had brought him down.

You would agree that here is the story of a man of the greatest courage and strength of character, a picture of self-sufficiency. All his life he had been fighting against adversity, and with some con-siderable success. Why, then, should he fail when effort seemed to offer its greatest rewards?

He came to me bcause of his inability to meet people, and what he described as 'a terrible inferiority complex'. He was apathetic, tense. He said he was afraid of the future, and that there appeared to be a huge mountain in front of him whatever he did. He was highly sensi-tive, always taking offence, and believing people to be set against him. He was restless, scrupulous, and sulky with his wife and family. At times he would quarrel with anyone on the slightest pretext, and it was this unhappy tendency that shattered all his efforts to secure employment. A childhood such as his could not fail to leave grievous scars behind, and it was the effect of the early years that caused his undoing in middle-life.

He arrived in the world an unwanted child, and this we can well understand for his mother resented the responsibility of the many children with which her drunken and absentee husband had burdened her. The atmosphere of the world into which the baby was born was one of fear, bitter hate, and physical violence. It is amazing that a child could make so much good out of a beginning like that.

Melanie Klein[1] has shown how important it is for the child to feel that he has allies. When he feels that his father and mother have forsaken him he must have friends who will be on his side against his parents, and these friends mean everything to him. In Harry's case they were his many sisters. If there are no such friends available, a child usually invents imaginary ones, which we term 'familiars', and the child will give them names, will talk to them and become inseparable from them. It is impossible for a child to face life com-pletely alone, and remain whole at the same time, and in cases where allies are wanting the mind may be disintegrated by the intolerable

[1] Cf. *Narrative of a Child Analysis.*

situation. It was fortunate for Harry that he was the only boy among many sisters, so that it was easy for him to play the part of hero. But apart from this it was of the greatest importance to all the children that they felt themselves to be intimately bound together in a strong alliance. It was this that helped to keep those children sane.

I can remember a patient who told me that as a child her only ally was a teddy-bear. But this inseparable companion became so dirty and undone that one day her mother threw it on the fire. This was a shattering experience, for it meant that her mother had destroyed her one friend in the world, and the intensity of her experience sheds some light on the affection children have for their toys and their pets, whether animate or inanimate.

A second factor in the life of this remarkable man was his native courage. Without this his life-story would have been very different. Courage can have no expression unless there is danger, fear, or difficulty, and Harry's life was surrounded by these elements from the very beginning. Harry was truly courageous, as distinct from the fearless person, who may be foolhardy but never courageous.

From his very infancy Harry sensed his isolation, his severance from the creative source of living. He was an outcast and did not belong, and this primal fear, that enveloped him from his infancy, unconsciously resulted in measures being taken to cope with the intolerable emotional hurt. He evaded the basic difficulty, and adopted a role of utter self-sufficiency, but it was because of the evasion, which was carried into adulthood, that his life was undermined and disillusionment followed.

We shall not understand this life unless we see the depth of fear upon which everything was based. The first objects upon which he sought to depend, as every infant must, were uncertain if not emotionally hostile. He felt unsupported and alone at a time when life is not possible without support and firm relationships. And all that was left for him to do was to manage, as best he could, devoid of support and normal dependence upon people. Thus he organized himself to be independent as life unfolded before him, and he became increasingly self-reliant and self-sufficient. Since no one looked after him he would look after himself, and since there had been no one whom he could trust, he had to place his trust in himself alone. Since his world was uncertain, he became only certain of himself.

This ruling pattern of self-sufficiency was his defence against his ever present fear born of aloneness and unsupportedness. By his efficiency he protected himself against the fear and pain of helplessness, and he covered his sense of weakness by a flamboyant show of adequacy and self-reliance. He became meticulous and conscientious, made sure that he would be given full marks for reliability, and was careful to show an example to his fellows by his tenacity, hard work and ability. No wonder Harry was a man of merit and made rapid progress.

It is relevant at this stage to note, as Adler has shown, the extent to which every man needs to feel significant and of value. Harry's home was a disgrace, he and his family lived in notoriously filthy conditions, ragged and verminous, and Harry would feel the bitter shame of it all. This was a body-blow to his need of self-respect, and thus he needed to establish himself even more before the eyes of the world. Unconsciously he set about developing in himself the virtues that were admired by others—hard work, devotion to duty, and the like. But unfortunately these qualities were prized not because virtue was seen to reside within them, but simply in order to gain status, and to gain acceptance with his fellow men. His efforts were therefore fundamentally insincere, and his achievements merely superficial. His ladder-climbing brought him no satisfaction whatever, for each rung only pointed to one higher up. But in middle-age, when it was becoming no longer possible to climb any higher, Harry fell to the ground, undone, his disillusionment complete. His system of living was destroyed 'in the twinkling of an eye,' and even 'all the king's horses and all the king's men could not put it together again.'

It is interesting at this point to consider the extent to which an uncontrollable upsurge of fear may have made Harry withdraw from his last promise of promotion, the fear that having accepted this promotion he might not succeed in the new and exalted sphere. Then instead of demonstrating his significance to the world he would be demonstrating his inadequacy. This possibility was too pregnant with too much potential shame to be risked, and the only course open was to take refuge in illness, with its additional possibilities of self-consolation and excuse. Harry's breakdown in middle-life occurred because the artificial defences, which he had managed to maintain, at great cost, throughout his life, failed at last and fear broke through. He failed because he was still in the grip of the fears that found their origins in his infancy, fears that arose from a profound sense of unsupportedness, rejection and isolation, and after a lifetime of struggle he found that he could no longer hold them at bay, for the old protective self-sufficiency had failed him for ever. It is no wonder that he felt that a mountain confronted him at each stage of life's journey, that he could no longer face the future, nor continue to maintain a normal relationship with people.

As a result of this sense of rejectedness and aloneness he felt deeply and painfully hurt, for he had been wronged beyond measure. Thus he indulged both in deep self-pity, and in smouldering rage. He was angry with life, angry with his parents, angry with everyone, for when he needed bread he was given a stone, and instead of fish, a scorpion. He felt unprotected, cold and unsupported, and we can understand his imagining everyone to be set against him. But the unfortunate result of this was that all his achievements were angry achievement, as it were in the face of people, defiant, assertive. And when people, quite naturally, did not take kindly to this he felt increasingly rejected and inferior, and justified in believing the world to be biased against him.

He complained of great tiredness, due in part to his defensive anger, but perhaps even more to his untiring efforts to sell himself to people. His expenditure of effort on this latter account must have been fantastic. His basic fear made it impossible for him to relax for a moment, and thus since he lacked the ability to allow life just to carry him along he could know no inner peace.

In their train, of course, these factors brought yet further bitterness and resentments. Why should he be having to drive himself like this? Why were the joys of life denied him, whilst others had their freedom? Thus there arose within him a secret rebellion against his own contrived effort and drive towards self-sufficiency, a conflict in which two forces were pulling him in opposite directions at the same time, one towards renewed effort, the other towards ease.

Obviously anything which undermined the pressures which he exerted upon himself in his endeavours to keep the basic fears at bay, only served to release those fears. Thus deep within himself would be the desire to relax the strenuous efforts that he had maintained over the long years, but this very desire, even though not consciously expressed, filled him with a strange apprehension which he could not understand, but which resulted in yet greater drive and renewed efforts. The crisis finally arrived when he was faced with the prospect of being promoted to the rank of colonel. The detached observer would have seen this prospect as one for which Harry was ideally suited, for he had throughout his life shown those very qualities of conscientiousness, attention to detail, and capacity for sustained work that would make him a first class senior officer. But Harry himself was being dragged in two diametrically opposed directions. Basically there was the temptation to take his ease after a life time of striving, and this would have led him to decline an offer of promotion. On the other hand if he did relax and release some of the pressures that he had exerted upon himself, then he would have to face the fears that he had suppressed since his infancy. Should he relax, or should he climb yet another rung in the ladder of promotion? The choice between the two alternatives was one that he could not make, for the emotional stresses and strains involved in the dilemma brought him to the point of breakdown. The conflict in which he found himself was too great to be lived with, his only solution was to retreat completely from the situation, and in so doing he sacrificed all the material rewards, such as increased salary and guaranteed pension in retirement, that should have recompensed him for a life time spent in the service of the army.

It needs little imagination to realize something of the distress that this whole episode, forming as it did the climax of a life's misdirected efforts, must have caused Harry, and the first step in the healing process was to try, patiently and quietly, to realize the tangle of emotional stresses that underlay the conflicts that had marred his life at almost every step.

I have presented you with a picture of colossal expenditure of life, an expenditure that was false in every respect, since it was designed to gain a place in the world by relying on unworthy reasons. Harry knew no creative joy, no sense of being a fellow worker with the Spirit, nor of God working through him. Any achievement had to be his, and his alone. 'By the might of mine arm have I gotten me . . . all this' (*Deuteronomy* VIII, 17). It would be easy to say that his sin was pride, but this was no wilful organization of his life. The truth was that the circumstances of his infancy, over which he had no control, had brought about a pattern of responses that had dogged his entire life, and the explanation of it all came to him as a penetrating and transforming revelation. We would not say that in his life he had exhibited the sin of pride, yet this Colossus of self-sufficiency was as remote as could be from that way of life that finds expression in the statement 'my sufficiency is of God.' He was his own Almighty God, creating and moulding his own world. Life, however, would not permit him to succeed in this, hence his illness.

Strangely enough, there is a truth in his distorted and exaggerated pattern, for we do need to feel strong, albeit our strength is of God. Our souls demand strength, support and encouragement, and we are never meant to go through life feeling ashamed, weak and inferior.

Perhaps the story of Harry can be summed up in no better way than by quoting the words of T. S. Eliot, written for Becket, in *Murder in the Cathedral*:

> 'The last temptation is the greatest treason,
> To do the right deed for the wrong reason.'

CHAPTER 3

AUTHORITY AS AN ENEMY OF LIFE

I

The dictionary defines authority as 'power', 'the right to enforce obedience.' It carries weight, and weight can become a burden. It exerts pressure upon us. Sometimes people come to me complaining of a weight upon their heads, or upon their chests or shoulders, or perhaps they are conscious of a constant pressure which they may describe as stress or tension. These various experiences may well have their origin in authority which has been felt to be an enemy of life.

No one, of course, from the Queen to her humblest subject, is free from authority, and thus the fully integrated life is not one which has not experienced authority but one which has experienced the right kind of authority and has come to terms with it. Our Lord was impressed by the man who not only exercised authority but also felt himself to be under it (*St Mark* VIII, 9–13). His manner was authoritative:

> 'And they were astonished at his doctrine: for he taught them as one that had authority, and not as the scribes.'   (*St Mark* I–23.)

while it was said of the Christ Child that He was subject to His parents:

> 'And he went down with them, and came to Nazareth, and was subject unto them.   (*St Luke* II–51.)

It should also be noted that just previously, at this age of twelve, he had exhibited an independent mind to an extraordinary degree:

> 'And he said unto them (his parents) How is it that ye sought me? wist ye not that I must be about my Father's business? And they understood not the saying which he spake unto them.'

The dangers with regard to authority in a person's formative years are two fold. First, there may be too much authority, rigorously imposed. The frequent result then is that the child, in reaching adulthood, is not able to call his life his own and serious reactions follow. Secondly, there may be too little authority in the early years, and as the person develops he may be unable to express himself freely and

C   33

fully within the confines of the normal framework of life within which all of us must live in society. A child may become pathologically insecure on account of not having experienced sufficient authority.

Insight into many personal problems reveals a struggle with authority and its numerous entanglements. The dream often reveals 'the authority complex', to which we are guided by a variety of symbolic figures, that of the policeman being doubtless the most common. Other such figures are the Seer, the Saviour, the Wise Old Man, the Good Mother; these and other similar figures are beneficial aspects of authority, and they work for the dreamer's good. The sinister aspects of the problem of authority may appear under the symbolism of the Judge and the Jailer, the Devil, and the Witch and similar figures.

People often ask what are the characteristics of good authority that distinguishes it from bad authority, and the answer is that in the case of those positive forms, that are in themselves expressions of freedom, the pressure does not come wholly from without but comes also from an inner approval and acceptance. Thus the authority of respect is something that we give ourselves; the authority of genuine gratitude is something that we ourselves feel spontaneously; the authority of reason is something we perceive. These are all good and creative attitudes, they come from within and they carry their own inner weight.

Peter Fletcher, in his recent book *Emotional Conflict*, illustrates the part authority and discipline play in life by one approach when teaching a child to ride a bicycle. He says, 'Your authority is the grip you maintain on the saddle to prevent the bicycle from going too fast or too far before the boy can control its speed and direction. Your discipline is the strength you use to restrict your pupil's freedom of action at a point where he is in danger of losing it; that is, when otherwise he would lose his balance and fall off. But your pupil does not fear your authority, or resent your discipline, because he knows, and he knows you know, that you impose restraints for the purpose of enabling him to do without them. From the start to the finish there is mutual understanding and intelligent co-operation in the common pursuit of a consciously shared aim.'[1]

This apt illustration shows the dangers of the two extremes. Where there is too little control then, in the terms of the illustration, the child may have a serious accident. On the other hand where there is too great control the stage may never be reached where the child is

[1] p. 37.

able to dispense with the authority and ride freely and adventurously, within the limits laid down by the mechanics of the machine.

The child deprived of authority and its attendant disciplines may be expected to become anti-social, for he has been given the impression that the universe was made for him alone, and given this attitude he naturally reacts against discipline. It appears to him that people are always interfering with his rights, being deliberately hostile to his best interests. Thus he is quite ready to take the law into his own hands, and without a twinge of conscience will raid a bank, cosh the custodian and anyone who attempts to impede him, and then he justifies himself by feeling that he is only taking what is his due, and that he is, in fact, being true to himself in an act of self-determination. In many cases of such anti-social behaviour I should expect to find a history of lack of authority and discipline in upbringing, or the behaviour may be the expression of deep-seated rebellion against an authority that was excessive. Needless to say this is not invariably the case and there are in addition cases of anti-social behaviour due to culpable wilfulness, or to extreme discouragement in childhood, as when a child is given *neither* help *or* understanding whilst battling with a natural intellectual disability.

When Lord Acton said 'All power tends to corrupt, and absolute power corrupts absolutely,' he was using a statement that could well be applied to authority, for authority is power. We hate dictatorships, with their absolute power, because they corrupt absolutely, and what they corrupt is human freedom. To many a small child the parent is seen as a dictator, as the enemy of his free development, and thus a threat to his existence as a person. The child senses that he is being denied the right to be himself, and life is never worth living unless *we* live it.

Excessive authority in childhood can result in two possible behaviour patterns. First, there are those who, perhaps after a very long struggle, capitulate and from there on comply with their authorities. We shall discuss this reaction later, but in this first part of the chapter we are concerned with those who, in a desperate attempt to be free, rebel against all who would control them. They may vainly think that by this rebellion they are gaining their freedom, but the fact is otherwise, since no one would rebel against anything which meant nothing to him, and the rebellion only shows the power authority holds. In our own case, whenever we react against an order, perhaps wanting to do the very opposite, we demonstrate our own fear of authority and its power over us.

The great damage is done to the child's personality when he is crushed by parental authority, and this factor may well contribute to, if not create, one of the frightful obsessional disorders. Apart from this, it may produce the type of person who invariably has to go against the government, the man who always has a grievance, because he feels life to be set against him. These people are very angry with every form of authority, since they rebel on principle. They put up a show of strength, and, like Nietzsche, they despise weakness which surrenders to authority, and shows of strength are the order of every day. They bow to no man, because they see everyman as a potential threat to their freedom. They are lonely because they see everyone intent upon interfering with their rights, and withdraw from them in self-defence. They are anxious because of their deep fear, for despite their shows of bravado they feel themselves to be basically weak.

Such people are ruled by fear, the fear of authority, and those who are committed to the healing ministry must undertake the difficult task of delivering them from their fear. As soon as they can face authority and deny its right to control them, then they are free. After they have gained this freedom, then they may well take a second look at authority, and say, as doubtless would the Prodigal Son, 'after all it was reasonable to expect this from me,' and they accept it all with grace. This acceptance is totally different from the original imposition for it is *they* who now freely accept, no longer are they being coerced and dominated by an external power. Authority is only good for us when we see its rightness and freely accept it, and there is no virtue whatever in a puppet-like response to a command.

All this has an obvious relevance to our religion, which can be presented with a threat, and a reminder that God has power to cast us into the everlasting fires of Hell. Our minds go back to the mediaeval painters who portrayed the flames of Hell above the chancel arch for a perpetual warning to the congregation—and there is no need to mention certain Old Testament attitudes that involved the same approach. So long as the appeal is to fear it will prevent the free response of people, and will be based upon the declaration that might is right. Fear is the most primitive emotion and to use this in God's name and in His service is to try to establish the best by an alliance with the worst, which is what our Lord refused to do in the third temptation. (*St Matthew* IV, 8–10.) We cannot agree with John Keble that we can be saved by fear as well as by love,

'Let us not miss the accepted hour:
Save, Lord, by love or fear.'

for though we may be frightened into correct behaviour, correct behaviour does not save us, as we shall be seeing in a later chapter. An appeal to fear is devoid of value because it is inseparable from compulsion, and self-seeking. It disallows a free and true expression of the self, so that it is no wonder that people have rebelled against religion in the name of freedom! To quote Peter Fletcher again : 'Coercion does not educate, it can only condition,' and to have the right conditioned reflexes according to a religious pattern carries no virtue whatever. The kind of authority which creates a mechanical response is but a form of brain washing, and against this every fibre of our being should rebel, for it is indeed something to be afraid of.

The importance of the deliverance from Egypt, 'the house of bondage', which is never forgotten in the Bible, is just the deliverance from an enslaving authority, with its power to compel to make bricks, and more bricks, and bricks without straw. The deliverance declared that God is the God of Freedom, and it has been a sad day for religion whenever God has been made into another Pharoah. Christ came to deliver us from the fear and power of such, by a mightier salvation than that of Egypt. He calls us into the service of His perfect freedom.

Let me now illustrate what I have been trying to establish from the life stories of people who have come to me for help. The first is Geoffrey, who for the first years of his life fell under the direct power of a Pharoah, in the person of his grandmother. His mother was completely enslaved to her. The grandmother believed that severity was good for a child, and that in no way should he be pampered. She saw to it that her matriarchal ideas were enforced upon the child. The father was away on military service for long periods, and on the rare occasions when he put in an appearance he insisted that this child of his should in no way disturb his peace and enjoyment. The crying of the little child was particularly irritating to him, and the impression created in the child was of one who stood above him threatening. Although that child is now a man in the mid-forties he readily raises his arm to shield his face from an unseen hand, and he is fear-ridden, angry, and wildly rebellious against authority.

He once pictured himself as a child in a corner, while before him was a huge ape-like man with a great cudgel set with many long nails. Everytime he made to advance from the corner the cudgel was raised and would have struck him. Authority had, of course, completely trapped and immobilized him in life, so that in mid-life he still feels as helpless as he did when a small child. What he would like to do with that beast in front of him beggars description, and he seeths with repressed rage.

You will not be surprised to hear that in religious matters he is a rebel. He is intensely angry with God, Whom he sees as One who takes delight in destroying him. He is the fly whose wings God is slowly tearing off, and this terrible image of God has been formed in his mind as the result of the authority exercised in his home.

He cannot understand the Church of England's attitude towards worship. It appears to be a most distasteful exercise. He much prefers the way in which one can walk around in Roman Catholic churches on the Continent, and come and go freely during the services. This appeals to him because thereby he could show his hidden anger towards and contempt of the High and Almighty God. He is not going to bow before Him, nor submit to Him in any way. Humility is something he simply cannot understand; it is an expression of weakness and deserves all it gets. He admired the Napoleons of history, who strike out against the powers about them, and in fantasy he had put himself upon the throne of the universe where he would submit neither to God nor man. 'I bow to no man,' he told me, and he would as easily add 'and to no God.' Yet his basic fear of authority binds him to God, and his fear of Him is matched by his anger towards Him, Whom he sees as the arch enemy of his freedom.

On one occasion he said to me: 'God is dangling me on the end of a string like a puppet. This is everlasting torture, this is what Hell is. I am the Wandering Jew, condemned to everlasting torment.' During analysis his mind turned to the Waters of Bitterness which he longed to have sweetened by throwing in a tree,

> 'And when they came to Marah, they could not drink of the waters of Marah, for they were bitter; therefore the name of it was called Marah (bitterness). And the people murmured against Moses, saying, What shall we drink? And he cried unto the Lord; and the Lord showed him a tree, which when he had cast into the waters, the waters were made sweet . . .' (Exodus XV, 23-24.)

He associated with this tree a Cross. The association of a Cross with the material thrown up in a dream or fantasy is always a healthy sign, for the Cross has the power to transform bitterness and hate, to heal grief and a sense of futility.

The Cross in common speech is descriptive of any burden which has to be carried, and in this sense the self-pitying hysteric uses it. 'How badly life has treated me!' But the true significance of this aspect of the meaning of the Cross is that it calls for utmost creative activity in man, which combined with the help of God, can transform a defeat into a victory, a 'hard-luck story' into an account of a man who, like Mark Tapley, 'has come out strong'.

At the stage of the analysis under consideration, the fleeting association appeared to have no immediate effect, and Geoffrey's mind resumed its rancour and hopelessness. He commented that life

'Is a tale told by an idiot, full of sound and fury,
Signifying nothing.'

On one occasion he came to me with the details of a dream that he
had produced since the preceding session:

'It was a very windy night. The water boiler of my house was being
fanned by the wind, which caused the water to boil. I looked into the
fire and the intense heat. My wife said to me, "The water will be good
for washing".'

In the interpretation at which we arrived, the wind was the symbol
of the Spirit, as in the Nicodemus narrative:

'The wind bloweth where it listeth, and thou hearest the sound thereof,
but canst not tell whence it cometh, and whither it goeth: so is everyone
that is born of the Spirit.'   (St John III, 8.)

The windy night, besides representing the intense activity of the
recreative Spirit, could also have represented Geoffrey's wild spirit, a
sign of his tempestuous rage. His wife, in this case, represents the
instinctual and practical Good Mother, for she helps him to realize
that much washing needs to be done, and here is the cleaning water
all ready, as for a Baptism. She realized the possibilities for good that
lay within the situation, that the fire within him can be 'hallowed
and directed aright.'

This twisted wreck of a man, living in a daily Hell, had been largely
made what he was by stern authorities, and his repression of love and
his reaction of rage was his reply to his being deprived of his essential
freedom.

Another person who consulted me dreamt of a shrub being grafted
on to ivy. He was the shrub which should have enjoyed an independent life of its own. It is also significant that the plant with which
he was being associated was the ivy, which is so often associated with
memory, and is a poisonous plant which clings parasitically and destroys the life upon which it feeds. The dream was extremely rich in
symbolism, and analysis revealed that in this case a massive authority
was both the poison and the parasite, and his unconscious memory
was responsible for the destructive grafting of the authority to his
personality.

Finally I would like to tell you about Rachel, who is forty-one. I
knew her twenty-three years ago when she was suffering from strange
upsets and pains, and since those days her troubles have increased
both in number and intensity. Her latest development is epilepsy,

which was an exchange for migraine, though she reported other troubles too, such as depression with severe fatigue and disinterestedness, and a guilt complex, expressed in her repeated assertion 'It is all my fault.' She is most aggressive, saying at times most horrible things and going into uncontrollable rages, and she complains of various pains in the back of her neck, on her chest, and in her back. Two years ago she was found wandering the streets in a fugue state, and among her compulsions was a formula 'onions and carrots, banana and custard,' that she had to say before completing a shopping list. Moreover she had to follow a strict order in washing up the pots, and she could change very quickly from the depths of depression to feeling on the top of the world.

Before we consider some of these symptoms in greater detail let us try and focus them against her unhappy background. She felt her father to be remote and disinterested both in her and her two elder sisters. However the real trouble was her mother who deliberately prevented the father from being a real friend, by drawing the children away from him to herself. At the first interview this was all she could remember about her mother, save that there were frequent rows between her parents. The eldest sister was really mother to Rachel, whilst she hated the other sister for her bossiness.

It was later that she recalled how her mother used to threaten her, a constant refrain being 'If you are not a good girl . . . I'll . . .' this often being followed by a slap. She recalled a forgotten memory of being punished by being put into a dark cellar, in which she felt that there were witches with long fingers reaching out towards her in the darkness. For years after this her dark bedroom filled her with terror, for she was never allowed to have a night-light.

Rachel was an unwanted child, and sensing the emotional coldness of her world, she sought to find some way by which she could draw the maternal source of life to her. She hit upon illness as a means by which her mother's protective care could be found. But this did not pay very good dividends for her mother did not believe in illness, and Rachel said that when she was ill in bed her mother would almost throw her meals at her. Her mother would often say 'After all I have done for you!' whereupon Rachel would ask herself 'What has she done for me?' and then she would refuse to co-operate. Admittedly her mother supplied the essential material comforts, but she felt so remote from her mother that she could never ask her anything.

A further annoyance was the mother's attitude towards the middle daughter, who was gay, a veritable man-hunter. And this the mother encouraged by giving her endless parties. When the father protested the mother undermined his authority, saying, 'Don't take any notice of him.' In fact the mother deliberately opposed anything the father said, with the result that he lost all interest in the home, and used to go off for days on country rambles. This latter became one of the patterns of behaviour which Rachel adopted, for she, having repressed the need for love, and experiencing the sheer misery of the home, would get up in the morning before anyone else, go out for the day, and come home to bed. We have mentioned that she was found wandering the streets in fugue state, and this was but an intensification of the former method of escape, by means of daily rambles, from the impossible burden of her home.

Rebellion was her chief reaction to the cold domination of her mother in the early years. She was determined to have her own way, and to this end she said: 'I bullied, I used lies, I played up, and used any other means; nothing stopped me.' Whilst she was thus fiercely fighting for her own life she was also producing great guilt, which in its turn was repressed. Her unconscious conflict now became clear, for on the one hand she must obey the voice of authority, which, by the process of introjection, had become her own voice of conscience: but on the other hand she must rebel in order to live her own life and be free. In addition to this, her angry rebellion struck back at her, for a principle of life is that what we give that also we must receive; thus her anger became self-punishment, which was consciously experienced as depression.

One of Rachel's practical difficulties in later life was her inability to rise in the morning. We saw in this part of the same pattern of refusing the dictates of duty, and of rebellion against responsibility. Moreover, by this means she gave herself the good time which she felt due to her, and also it brought gratification to her aggressiveness to make difficulties for the rest of the family.

The extreme intensity of her anger was revealed both in the migraine and the epilepsy she suffered. We have to think of three stages in the expression of hostile emotions. The first is confined to fantasied attacks upon some object, but when these fantasies are inhibited, along with the hostility, migraine may be experienced. The second stage contains the hostile wish, again inhibited, but in this case the vegetative processes of the body are organized for the activity, and in this case hypertension may be the symptomatic expression. The final stage is when the necessary processes for specific action have been organized, and then the voluntary act is inhibited; and because this concerns muscular action its symptom is arthritic. Rachel's migraine, therefore, was the expression of her inhibited hostile fantasies.

We have already said that her migraine was later exchanged for what were diagnosed as epileptic fits. It would be in keeping with her history to find that her 'epilepsy' was pseudo-epilepsy, and this has been endorsed by the fact that, up to the time of writing, she has had no further attacks for a considerable period. These fits would then express her inability to face both the intolerable life situation, and the fantasied hostilities buried in her unconscious.

We have seen how in the past Rachel's living space was all too restricted, and that undue pressures were constantly exerted upon her. It was found that, although the conditions of her early life had naturally changed, unwittingly similar restrictions were still being imposed upon her. Her mother was constantly in her home 'helping', so much so that Rachel felt once more that she was being pushed out by her. Her husband, by trying to shake his wife out of her illness, was but assuming a new form of the old authority. The following dream revealed this aspect of her problem:

> 'A new house was being built (i.e. a new self), I felt I could not live in it for it was according to my husband's specification: it was far too cramped. Through the windows I could see the vast expanses of wonderful country.'

The meaning of the dream is self-evident in the context of Rachel's marriage. Her life has blossomed like the proverbial rose by the gaining of a hitherto unknown self-respect, by the removal of her present pressures, and her insight into what had so grievously distorted her life in the past.

Thus a few of the adverse effects that result when authority exerts excessive and crushing pressures have been outlined, and Isabella, in *Measure for Measure*, is surely right when she says:

> 'Tis excellent to have a giant's strength, but it is tyrannous
> to use it like a giant.'

At the beginning of the chapter some of the characteristics of good authority were discussed, and undoubtedly there are times when an external authority, even when utilizing pressure, is justified. But these authoritative pressures should always be temporary expedients, and should not be exercised a moment longer than is absolutely necessary. These pressures are brought upon a child to make him observe certain standards of behaviour which are, for example, consistent with road safety. But as soon as he sees the wisdom of this behaviour for himself then the pressures are removed. The rule is that the wise authorities should always be working to such an end that their external authoritative positions are no longer necessary. This is what St Paul meant when he said:

'The law was our schoolmaster to bring us to Christ.' (*Galatians* III, 24.) The aim being to take people beyond the law so that by their own good judgment and insight they would 'love the good and hate the evil.' John the Baptist represented an order of law when he said:
'He must increase, but I must decrease' (*St John* III, 30).

Unfortunately the authority that is necessary for the training in freedom has a power that is not always readily relinquished. In this way the authority of convention and tradition can become a stumbling block, and this can be seen in the relationship between Jesus on the one hand, and the Scribes and Pharisees on the other. They saw Him as One who rode roughshod over tradition, and they asked:

> 'Why do thy disciples transgress the tradition of the elders? for they wash not their hands when they eat bread. But He answered and said unto them, Why do ye also transgress the commandment of God by your tradition?' (*St Matthew* XV, 2–3, *St Mark* VIII.)

Authority for authority's sake is always destructive, and it is in this connection that the Authority of the Church has to be watched carefully. Christ saw authority in its creative and positive aspect, as deriving from insight and vision, whereas if the Church sometimes tends to exercise an external authority, then inevitably conformity becomes an exalted virtue. At a deep personal level too, authority in its various forms is incorporated into the conscience, and if the authorities are excessive and negative then the Super Ego can cause a wastage from scrupulosity, and torments of self-punishment, that are immense.

Good authority enables the child to develop into a mature person, free and responsible, the person who is the most law-abiding of citizens whenever the external law is seen to be an expression of life and love. Bad authorities, as St Paul said, 'gendereth unto bondage', whereas good authorities lead to that freedom that enables a full expression of life, one which loves, and because it loves does what it likes, and can do no wrong.

II

In the first part of this chapter we considered a very common reaction to authority, that of rebellion; now we shall consider the opposite response of compliance. I suppose that for most mothers there are two cardinal virtues, cleanliness and compliance. With what pride a parent would say, 'I have had no trouble with my children, they have always done what they were told.' These children may be models of conventional behaviour, scrupulous and conscientious, but on becoming adults they may be altogether incapable of taking responsibility, so meek and mild that no one ever notices them, and paralysed every time they are called upon to make a decision. They form the ignoble army of 'yes-men', Vicars of Bray, 'reeds shaken with the wind.'

Every dictator relies upon fear to bring people to heel, and such compliant people cause him not a moment's trouble, whereas the rest, the rebels, have to be liquidated. Authorities naturally put the stamp of approval upon the compliant, they are 'safe men', undeviating followers of the Establishment.

Such people are not likely to be aware of the fact that it is fear that dominates their every action and thought, and that it is authority which has cowed them into a permanent state of obedience. Long ago they lacked sufficient innate courage to be a Daniel and face the lions, and now they are anxiety-ridden. They have submitted to their authorities so completely that they can never permit their natural instinctual urges to find expression, and the rebel within them must be crushed whenever it rears its ugly head. This leads to the inhibition of vast energies which are God's gift to man and thus essential to fullness of life. Stekel[1] taught long ago that repression of instinct creates anxiety, and we find that these repressed and suppressed people are too anxious to sleep or play, work or worship.

Further, they are so dominated by authority, that authority itself lives their lives for them. They are used to being told at every turn how to act and how to think, with the result they have never been free to discover how to control and direct their own lives from within. A child never allowed to walk cannot walk, and a child never allowed to be independent cannot be independent. Children must be free to venture forth into the world, make mistakes, fall and stand up again, realizing they are still alive. This is the way to grow up, and it is to the great credit of the Prodigal's father that he did not exert his authority but allowed his son to leave home. If the child or young person is always held, controlled and directed, he can never learn by his own experience, and thus, in later years, he is too timid and inexperienced to take responsibility. Such people are often termed 'eternal infants', Peter Pans who do not want to grow up, and they are afraid of the world, and of life. What a cruel disservice has been done to them by authority, which has denied them their right to learn how to live. Quite often this effect is produced by parents who surround their children with their own anxieties, or who, by their over-senti-

[1] *Conditions of Nervous Anxiety.*

mentality, immobilize their children in life by surrounding them with a deadly kind of sentimental treacle.

Another form of control, both within the home and without, is the pernicious use of bribery, so that authority becomes established by the lure of rewards. 'If you are good I will give you a sweet' is a familiar enticement, and in the modern world the sweet is all too often material advantage—the capacity to earn £2,000 a year, 'provided you pass your examinations,' or the opportunity of 'getting on in the world, and keeping up with the Joneses,' but 'only if you pass your 11-plus examination.' Of course the promise of a merit holiday does not increase the pupil's love of being taught. But even more insidious is the fact that the child is subjected to promises in order to make him comply, and he will later despise himself for having accepted bribery. It is an underhand trick to make the child do the right thing for the wrong reason, and despite the fact that the child does the right thing, the behaviour is devoid of any real merit of any kind. It is a thoroughly bad situation for the child, and he will sense the dishonesty of it, for our personalities have a deep regard for honesty and sincerity. Trickery of this kind is bound to produce very hostile reactions and feelings of guilt at least in the unconscious.

A young man, who is also a very sick man, came to me for help. He had been an infant prodigy, and he knew the twelve times table up to twelve by the age of four, and at two he was able to carry on a conversation. The material he brings to his analytic sessions often concerns the most complex aspects of organic chemistry, and the latest developments in other fields of scientific knowledge. His mother trained him solely by reasoned argument, and today, as a young man, he can only operate in life along his mother's pattern, instinctual responses being almost completely suppressed. But life cannot be lived in this partial way, by means of the intellect alone. Thus many decisions that a fully integrated person would make smoothly, intuitively and with a minimum of stress, are subjected by this young man to exhaustive rationalization, almost inevitably with the result that the arguments are neither all in favour of, nor all against a particular course of action, and the result is an impasse. For example he has worked out an intricate series of logical tests, which require at least three months to complete, in order that, when he meets a girl, he can test whether in fact she is suitable for him. The result is quite obviously worthless, but as his authorities have never allowed intuition and feeling to play a part in his life, he knows no other standard of measurement.

Of course an able person can recognize intellectually that the emotions must play a significant part in life, and our young man did try to operate a kind of Box and Cox arrangement, using a sort of mental switchboard, whereby he could at times switch off his intellect and test a particular situation by use of his emotions. By switching back to his intellect he could then subject the same situation to rational tests, and the mean of the two results should give him his 'total response', that is the response that would be true for his complete personality. It need hardly be said that the system did not work. From his infant days only his rational self had been developed, and anything foreign to this aspect of himself was suspect. If he attempted to rely on the evidence of his non-rational self then his conscience worried him, and he hurriedly returned to the narrow confines of his intellect.

It became clear that during analysis that he had always had a deep interest in the police, and he said, 'I should have been a policeman.' In fact he had, of course, a private police force of his own special kind which kept much of his essential life in prison, and suppressed his instinctual urges. Such urges had to be submitted to the stern judgment of his warped conscience before being allowed into consciousness, and this warped conscience had contributed to his fractional personality.

Our young man has always been compliant for he felt that his mother, supported by his father, was too strong for him, and he said, 'If you can't beat them, join them.' However, somewhere within him there must still be a rebel that was repressed long ago, and our healing work is concerned with trying to find and revive this rebel. It must then be presented to the young man as something God-given and essential, and his new conscience must smile upon it and recognize the part that it must play in the whole man that he is destined to become.

Another person, forty-two years of age, came to me in a serious condition. She had a severe inferiority complex, and one of her complaints was that she looked 'like a pudding', and at times she would slap her face. She was a strong mixture of rebellion and rage on the one hand, and utter compliance and identification with people on the other, and this latter aspect was the dominant. Her personality was seriously split, and she often affirmed that she was not one person but two, and she did not know which of the two was her real self. Most often her attitude was cringing, and one of withdrawal, and she said that she 'was for ever running away.' She did not feel safe with people for she was afraid that they would 'suck out her life' and leave her 'dry and destroyed'.

Restless and insecure, ashamed and overwhelmed by a sense of her own essential badness, she was subject to fears of a most intensive kind. Thus she was afraid in a busy street, lest she might throw herself under a bus, and there were occasions when she wandered on to a very busy and fast road quite oblivious to any danger, and at night frequently she hung herself out from her bedroom window in a state of panic. Her physical symptoms included rashes in various parts of her body (symbolic of her deep sense of shame), palpitations and hay fever, claustrophobic feelings in houses and churches, and at times paralysis of her fingers.

Although part of her condition was of a very serious order, this lady provides a fairly typical example of someone who, as a child, found her authorities too strong for her, and with which she had eventually complied. Her authorities would have pressed in upon her from every side, but three aspects of the pressure revealed themselves to be particularly crippling and they might be considered in this discussion.

First, her mother, who was an invalid, suffering from hypertension, dominated the home, not in a physical way but emotionally. The kind of bind imposed upon the child is illustrated in the form of reproach to which all too often she was subjected, 'If you do other than what I want you to do I shall be hurt, and we all shall be hurt. And this you could not do, considering all we have done for you.' The simplest misdemeanours were met with pained expressions, and grim silences, so that she came to feel the meanest criminal, and became fearful least her sick mother might suffer and even die as the result of her own wicked naughtiness. Thus we find that as the child developed she grew to feel extremely dependent upon her mother, and because this dependence necessarily limited her own freedom there was in addition a great deal of hidden aggression towards her mother. The situation was further complicated by the fact that the home was a very religious one, and religion became absorbed into the mother's emotional authority, while in addition, the father who was a mild and sentimental man, was despised by the daughter for being a 'yes-man' to her mother.

Secondly, the mother's insistence upon the necessity of obeying all the social proprieties imposed an additional burden on the child. They lived in a very good district where people were most proper, and the paraphernalia of etiquette assumed gigantic proportions. The little child must conform to 'The Best' in everything, the best social conventions must be observed, she must meet only the best little girls, and at their parties do and say only the best things, she must be the best little girl in the best church of the best district. Anything less than the best pained and disgraced her parents. This made it most difficult for the child to build up healthy and natural relationships, and soon she went through agonies of mind whenever she was sent to a party, often escaping and running home, only to be greeted as though she had committed the crime of crimes. The emotional pressure was irresistible, the standard set impossible, and that standard she came to accept herself. Thus she came to disapprove of every suggestion within herself that was less than what she considered to be the best, and because these suggestions inevitably arose she was subjected to the tyranny of a bad conscience.

Thirdly, her elder sister was a grievous complication in the life of our small child, for she had mastered the art of doing the things her parents expected of her. She was the model child, ever praised and set up as an example, a paragon of virtues, and it is little wonder that she was envied and hated for her smug superiority. In fact the elder sister had eaten so deeply into the personality of our young child that even today, when she looks at herself in the mirror, she often sees not her own face but that of her sister. And as we follow the development of her life we find that discouragement reached such a point that hope was lost, and with this loss of hope life ceased to have any sense of purpose.

Part of her system of intense guilt, ruled over by her stern and uncompromising authorities embedded in her conscience, was based upon her relationship with her father. He frequently would set the little girl upon his knee and cherish her in what seemed to her to be a maudlin way, and today she is revolted by her father whenever she is in his presence. This emotional gush on her father's part, which may have been due to lack of erotic satisfaction in his relationship with his wife, inflamed the infants Electra Complex, and this she was incapable of resolving. Prior to this there had been unconscious fantasies regarding her father which had produced frequent vomiting attacks. The overall result was to be seen in her intense disgust with herself, and the shame which made her want to hide herself from mankind, and inflict upon herself severe punishments. Part of the punishment resulted in a conviction that she was utterly useless as a woman, and that she had brought this grievous state upon herself, for which she must suffer as long as she lived. She would not have experienced guilt so immensely had she not been surrounded by most stern and exacting authorities, which formed the system of her bad conscience (Super Ego), and thereby dominated her life.

Thus we have seen that our young child, at a very early age, became convinced that she was bad through and through. This resulted, in part, from the fact that her world, from the very beginning, ever demanded the impossible, and of course she could not meet its demands. She therefore viewed her apparent failure with feelings of great guilt, and her conscience lashed her unceasingly. Consequently there was a two fold aspect of her problem, her constant feeling of failure which led to a deep conviction of her own basic rottenness, and secondly her scrupulosity which was the product of her bad conscience. We find that today she cannot gain the slightest satisfaction from anything that she does, for she cannot believe herself capable of doing anything really worth while. When she is praised for her work she cannot accept it, and she says to herself, 'people are only saying this to boost me up.'

A particularly serious part of the problem under consideration was the fragmentation of the personality, the fact that she had been split into several selves. Her real self, which was related to her body, she was ashamed and afraid of, for she had come to feel that it was more than inadequate and socially unacceptable, that it was in fact corrupt and corrupting in every fibre. From this body of corruption she had sought to escape. Another form of her attempt to escape from her radical rottenness was, as has been mentioned, characterized by compliance and identification with other people, and so she had many false selves, which were made up from the requirements of other people. Her treatment as a child had led her to believe that if she was to be accepted it would be on the basis of what she did and how she behaved, but her bad demanding conscience condemned her behaviour, and she was filled with guilt. Therefore she rejected her true self. It thus followed that she had to live increasingly in her false selves, and they became so real that her true self became more and more remote and unknown to her. Hence her great difficulty in coming to terms with the real world.

In closing this discussion I will quote Peter Fletcher, 'Shakespeare is right when he says that "Conscience doth make cowards of us all," for more often than not what we call "conscience" is the inward echo of the voices of those who laid down the law when we were young and who visited our disobedience with punishment. It is this false conscience that causes us to indulge in orgies of self-praise or self-blame and makes us feel like a saint or sinner, proud or ashamed, according to whether what we do conforms to or breaks some rigid rule. If we feel that our personal worth can be measured up by reference to a fixed standard of conduct—religious, moral, social, intellectual or some other—we can be fairly certain that faulty training in habits of obedience accounts for many of our present emotional conflicts and nervous ills.'[1]

[1] p. 45

CHAPTER 4

THE BASIS OF LIFE

No one can ever be asked a more important question than 'What is your name?' If you can give a name in reply to that first question of the Catechism you have a very great possession, for to know your name is to be aware of your own identity, to be able to differentiate yourself from other people, and to feel that you possess your own life. Such an experience as this means that you have a real measure of freedom.

Two things are required to be a person with a name: first, a man must possess his own life, as it were, on the inside, and secondly, he must be related to other persons. It is obvious that a man will not be able to relate himself to anyone else unless he is authentically himself, yet he becomes himself only through relatedness to other persons. The statement of our Lord that 'the kingdom of God is within you' (*St Luke* XVII, 21) may have relevance here, for the kingdom is corporate, and yet it is within oneself; the community and the individual are inseparable from one another.

The infant in finding that the love he offers is received, and that the love of others comes to him, becomes capable of experiencing himself as himself, and others in relation to himself. When the interchange of love is only partially experienced, and worse still, when there is no experience of it at all, the most grievous of human problems are created. The infant feels that he has been given life, but he cannot live it; he is in a state of utter dependence, but there is nothing upon which he can depend. With one hand life is given to him and with the other it is taken away. Such experiences prevent the child from discovering his own name.

The significance of a name is illustrated in the first two chapters of St Luke's Gospel where the actual choice of a name is deemed to be of particular importance both in the case of John the Baptist, and Jesus. Many years followed before Jesus became fully conscious that His Name 'was above every name'. This realization gives the significance to His Baptism when the voice was heard saying, 'This is my beloved son, in whom I am well pleased' (*St Mark* I, 11). That event was His confirmation, His recognition, and it was an experience both within Himself and from without. If our Lord was like us, as we are told, then this confirmation would need to be repeated as His life unfolded before Him, and thus we may interpret his repeated acts of communion with the Father, and in particular the Transfiguration (*St Luke* IX, 28ff.).

No child, as indeed no adult person, with very few exceptions, can face life without being repeatedly confirmed by the people about him. He needs to feel, in order to grow up towards maturity, that he is socially acceptable. He is confirmed and thereby established in his essential self-esteem as he receives, day by day, encouragement and approval. Adler rightly placed very great importance upon the child being given encouragement, and he showed the bad effects of discouragement upon the development of the child. When confirmation is withheld the child is weighed down by feelings of inadequacy and inferiority with the result that he retires from responsibility. In some cases it may contribute to a questioning as to whether he is a self, and to the question 'Who am I?'

Another reaction to the lack of confirmation may be the repression of the need to be confirmed, and, as we saw in the second chapter, a person may replace it with a pose of self-sufficiency, which inevitably leads to shattering disillusionment. Most of us would readily admit that we live as we do because we receive a daily measure of confirmation, by means of social intercourse, or the acceptance of our love and work. The darkest times are when confirmation is withdrawn, and we are desperately alone; as when we most need a confirming voice from heaven and 'there was no voice, nor any that answered.' The intense pain of non-recognition was experienced upon the Cross, when our Lord's supreme act of faith went dis-confirmed. Thus He died, and it was only on the third day that the confirmation came. Such dis-confirmation destroys the hope by which we live, which is hope in ourselves, and in the responsiveness of the world around us; and it brings about a feeling of intense helplessness and loneliness in being confronted by a dangerous and confusing world.

Martin Büber says, 'a society is human in the measure in which its members confirm one another.' The Christian society confirms its members through its repeated declarations of forgiveness, and above all, in Holy Communion, the Love-feast and the expression of togetherness with God and man. I have been told many dreams in which the long table of Leonardo's fresco appeared, and these dreams carried the emotional quality of acceptance and strengthening by God and His early community. The Confirmation Service is the culmination of the individual's own seeking and the Divine response. The Church is always offering confirmation to her faithful people, and each member is called upon to confirm others in the Christian Way.

A simple experience of the dis-confirmation of which we have been thinking may be that of the traveller abroad who has forsaken the well-beaten track and who finds himself amongst people with whom he cannot communicate because of 'a confusion of tongues'. Again, it may be felt when a person is uncertain regarding his place in a social group, or more severely when the people around him are felt to be critical to the degree of being hostile. When this is experienced in a factual way, as when, for example, a person is 'sent to Coventry' by his work-mates, the hurt may be altogether unbearable, and the person may be driven to suicide. We should expect the depth of feeling in this case to be due to the situation recalling and re-activating the utterly unbearable separation from the source of life in infancy. Something akin to this may be experienced by the people who feel that they have committed 'the unforgiveable sin', for in this state they feel themselves to be no longer recognized by God or man, and they are totally without confirmation and all communication has broken down. This is a psychological condition, and you may have discovered how it is quite impossible to persuade such people to change their minds. It is worth remembering, in trying to help such people, that the emotional appeal of the Cross may bring them out of this sad state, that is if their emotions can be tuned in to the same wave-length. God's greatest act of confirmation was given on Calvary, for it is a confirmation which is given quite regardless of human merit, it is an absolutely free gift. It was the gift of acceptance to sinners, for it was being freely offered to the very people who placed Christ upon the Cross, to the thieves beside Him, to the faithless disciples, and to the murderers with their hate and scorn beneath Him.

Dr P. D. Laing[1] has shown how the lukewarm responses of parents fail to authenticate the child in his struggle to be himself. The child may feel ignored because the parents are actually disinterested in him, or just because they are too busy, or perhaps it may be because they believe that 'children should be seen and not heard.' We need not be surprised if then the child is driven to all kinds of exhibitionistic excesses, which will only make matters worse for these will be met with 'appropriate' treatment by the parents. There is also what has been called 'the tangential response', this is when the child expects confirmation, but instead of giving it the parent or teacher goes off at a tangent, and the value of the exercise to the child is completely lost, and the end is discouragement and dis-confirmation. The responses, which mean so much to the child, may be only a smile, a touch, or a simple word.

There are other occasions when it is most important to recog-

---

[1] *The Self and Others*, Ch. viii.

nize the child's good intentions, the expression of which may be catastrophic from the parents' point of view, as when the small child plucks off the heads of his father's prize chrysanthemum as a present for him. It is obviously most difficult on such occasions for parents not to be angry, but if they can restrain themselves the gain to the child will make it well worth while.

It is sad that children often feel themselves only confirmed when they put on a particular act or adopt a certain pose, in order to comply with the requirements of the people about them. In such cases it is only the false self that is confirmed whilst the real self is seen as a liability, and if this takes place in early life and persists serious splitting of the personality will result, as Dr Laing[1] has so clearly shown, and the person's real name will become less and less known, until finally it may be forgotten altogether.

Parents should also been seen to confirm one another in the eyes of the child, although there is a pitfall here, for very special care should be taken to see that the child is included in, and not excluded from, their confirmation. Where there is a mutual confirmation within the family, life is experienced as something of a balanced whole, 'it is fitly joined and knit together,' and because in this confirmation due respect is given to the individuality of each member, each one of them will hold his individuality, and know and possess his own name. Unfortunately all too often such conditions do not obtain, and, to illustrate this, I now propose to tell you about several people who were seriously hurt by this very thing.

Richard was a sensitive type of person about thirty years of age who came to me on account of his asthma. Although he was a deeply religious person he felt unable to deal with a spiritual bitterness of which he complained, and moreover he was quick to take offence and he had sadistic trends. He found it difficult to feel himself accepted, and yet he did not want acceptance; he was angry and aloof. You will notice his lack of confirmation as we consider his story.

His mother died when he was a fortnight old. His first attack of asthma appeared when he was two-and-a-half years old, and it was at this time that his father re-married. He felt that his childhood was not evenly secure. He described his step-mother as 'moody and unstable, possessive, hard, brittle and materialistic.' He was happy with his father, except when he felt angry with him for siding with his step-mother against him, although he was almost as angry on the many occasions when his father just withdrew and did nothing about

[1] *The Divided Self.*

an issue. This gave the boy a feeling of being unsupported, unprotected, alone; that is, he was unconfirmed by both his parents.

He was told that he would go to Hell if he were naughty. When he was four and five years of age he had a nanny who was obsessed with thoughts of the Devil and frequently spoke about him. On one occasion she blackened her face and pretended to be the Devil and the child was so frightened by this apparition that he leapt through a window. He went about in daily terror of the Devil and he was for ever wondering whether his behaviour warranted his being carried off by him, and thus he could never be sure of the outcome of his actions and his thoughts. This uncertainty and suspicion of himself increased his lack of confirmation. It is no wonder that he had doubts regarding himself, and that he used to ask 'Who am I?'

A piece of free writing revealed both his natural desire for venture and freedom, and the ever watchful and critical eye (of the Devil) upon such self-expression. He wrote:

'Riding a tricycle . . . Where've you been? Don't care; it was good while it lasted. Always wanted a bike to tear about on, to knock about. Sorry, mine got knocked about, but there it is! Whoosh! Over the hump, skidding, our grave! Crash! Hurt! but all part of the risk. Freedom of movement. To be wild was to be free to shriek and shout in God's air. Remember two old hens at the bus stop. Tear ahead on bike. Fast, careless and shrieking. Saw them look at me with a "what's the world coming to" stare. Go, go, shriek and yell—round the corner and up over. The copse—*ours*—the farm. Father backing out of drive in Austin car. Struggling, anxious, timid. Has his own problems—perhaps too many . . . for me! Sits in arm chair—reading, relaxing. Distant. Doesn't really know me. Nothing really in common except that he's "Dad". Sitting room/dining room. Winter's evening. Fire. Mother pottering about doing odd things. No contact other than she's there.'

On account of his step-mother's remoteness, his father was the only possible person he could approach, but repeatedly help was refused, or his father was too immersed in his own problems, as the above writing shows. This made the child feel very angry; he was betrayed, deprived of support, which made him face a very difficult world without support. He was a fish out of water gasping for air, which his asthma well revealed. He was denied his individual significance and freedom of movement, and although he had all the material comforts he could wish for, that which he wanted most of all was lacking, love. The over-attention which his step-mother gave him was devoted to anything but himself as a person, and the more she dominated his life and swamped him in protective care, the more he gasped and choked.

Richard longed to be of real use in the world, to do things which really mattered, and to find himself accepted in them, but here again, he found himself unestablished. He asked his father if he might help him in the cleaning of the car, but he was told there was no room for two people in the garage. He wanted to help in the mowing of the lawn, but that should be left to the one who knew best how to do it. The result was that the boy said to himself, 'When I'm free I'll never trust myself to anyone,' and 'The closer I am to a person, the more likely I am to be hurt.' This frustrated desire to express himself in a way acceptable to others led to a withdrawal, and to the anger behind his asthma. His unconscious desire to be accepted became exaggerated, and it developed into a conscious desire to force himself upon people through domination. This grew to such an extent that it frightened him, which also contributed to his putting a distance between himself and other people. The result of all this was that he did not give other people a chance to confirm him, he denied himself of what he wanted most of all.

Another person said, 'Whatever I did there was something wrong in it. I had no foothold anywhere.' Someone else as a very small child was told to go to Granny's for tea after leaving school. She forgot this instruction and went home only to find the house locked and empty, whereupon, in a panic, she ran to the Granny's house, where, instead of sympathy and comfort, she received a most frightful scolding. She was told that she was 'the most careless and thoughtless child ever.' Commenting generally upon her early years she said, 'all the people about me were so very frightening. They gave immense punishments for the slightest faults. I never seemed to do anything right.' In fact, she was given no confirmation.

The child must feel himself respected, and then he will respect himself, otherwise he may doubt who or what he is. The young man previously mentioned said that as a child he was given no assurance that he, as a person, had any value. When he came home for the school holidays, after being away for some three months, his step-mother's first remarks were regarding his suit; she would carefully examine it, whilst he, inside the suit, appeared to be of neither interest nor consequence. The things about him mattered more than he did.

Another man, who in his early years had lacked confirmation, said, 'My value is in the hands of others, I have no inner value of my own. Life is a desperate game, with threats of ruin all the while.' This was because he felt to be nothing within himself, and in order to cover up this feeling he drove himself mercilessly lest he should be ruined for life, and at the same time he tried to withdraw from people. He could never talk amongst people in a group, and he said the only time he felt safe was when his mother was backing him up. She had to confirm him moment by moment, for the damage to his personality had already been done. He produced an interesting dream.

'I was in bed and my mother was bringing me the morning cup of tea. A man came in and I wanted him to pick up the empties. He was quite nasty about it.'

There he was having retreated from life, expecting his mother to do everything for him; he was there to be ministered to. He expected his father to do likewise, but he was rightly showing disapproval. He had gone to bed, which symbolized a return to mother, because he had found life too difficult without confirmation, he was too un sure of himself to face the world. 'The waves of the sea were mighty and raged horribily,' but deep within himself there was no stability, nothing which could ride the storm. The father in the dream would represent the Good Father, the wise guiding authority, who by his disapproval was helping 'his son' towards a better attitude towards life, in fact behind the apparent sternness was a hidden act of confirmation, for he was virtually saying, 'You *can* do better than this, you are worth more than this.'

Having spoken about the importance of confirmation, we shall consider another factor which can destroy the basis upon which a full life must be built. It is when the child's achievements are assessed as being of greater worth than the child himself. He is led to believe that his value lies in his passing the 'eleven-plus' examination, or in his obtaining a scholarship. In the case of the girl of a certain social background her value may be presented to her as consisting in her ability to create a good impression. What she is herself as a person seems not to matter in the least, whereas her deportment, her social tact, her airs are far more important than herself.

The roots of this serious distortion of life, which hides from a person his essential self, are to be found in the toilet training of infancy, when what the child does either makes him loved and accepted, or casts him into the outer darkness when he performs at the wrong time or in the wrong place, or does not perform at all. This interpretation of life is later confirmed in a thousand ways, for the parents have such set ideas as to what is right or wrong, and such dreadful consequences follow upon wrong action, that all that matters is what one does. It is obvious how this appraisal of what is 'good' lays itself open to tempting the child to practise all manner of deceits in the interests of *doing* the right things.

As the time passes on the child naturally wants to do things, and his games are important adult activities in miniature, and also by this activity he attracts attention of one kind or another, for even bad behaviour has a certain kind of value in that it attracts notice of people. The means is always by the *doing* of things. Everything goes to confirm him in this view, for all his little exploits are carefully noted, his first steps, his first words and attempts at writing, these like all other things done assume a colossal importance. It is no wonder that the child attaches value only to what he does.

Later on, as a schoolboy, he has to face the report upon his activities and how he has worked during the past term; rarely is there anything much in the report about his development as a person. The post-mortem upon the report goes to confirm that his sole value is his place in the form or his prowess on the field of sport. When the day comes for him to leave school he enters a world which appears to measure everything by the same yardstick, and he becomes what is described as 'successful' in his business or profession, and when he comes to die he will again be measured by what he has done. The newspapers will declare what he was worth in so many pounds. We may smile, but it is the way in which most of us assess our value and that of others all through life. The value, the real deep abiding value, of everyman is not in what he does, but in what he *is*. Our Lord took such interest in the common people because He did not measure their worth in the things they possessed but in what they were as persons. A person's sins or guilt had to be dealt with but He penetrated deeper than these to the person who was there beneath the sins and errors. It has been an ever present temptation to be more concerned with sins than with sinners—perhaps the sins are more interesting to us !

In Everyman there is the central and all important person, some-one unique and unrepeatable; and when people feel this about them-selves they will have a basis upon which a full and satisfying life can be built. Therefore we should so deal with children that they feel themselves to be infinitely more important than their clothes, or being clean, or the report they bring home from school. When the child appears to be the biggest failure he most needs to be assured of his value as a person, that he is loved in spite of his actions.

I will tell you about a young lady who suffered much from this kind of thing, without mentioning the very serious aspects of her illness.

Her father was a generous kind of person, yet he was one of those people who drives everyone, whose pattern of life was somewhat like that of Harry in the second chapter. It must be said out of fairness to him, that he tried to do the best possible for his family, but he became a slave to the immense pattern of work which he created. The result was that the only expression of love came to be his work, the one and only measure of value was work. The whole family were caught up in a whirlwind of activity, and each one of them became captivated by work. It became a sin to be at ease, and a criminal offence to be idle. The father was one of those rare people who only needed three hours of sleep a night, and more than once he was known to work thirty-eight hours without taking any rest at all.

Thus the family became a great machine, where the values were hard work and efficiency. Significance could only be had by means of work, with the result that the whole family became depersonalized; and had no value as persons. The daughter, whom we are considering, said, 'I am nothing,' and we can easily appreciate her feeling in this way. Inevitably there built up in her unconscious a vast ocean of resentment, bitterness and hate, and this expressed itself in an unconscious opposition to work; thus she said, 'There is never any satisfaction in what I do,' and work became increasingly difficult to do, and yet she knew consciously that she could have no significance apart from work. Further, an element of rivalry entered the scene on account of her being a younger member of the family. She accordingly became envious of those who could do more than she could. The big brothers were so much stronger, and they were close to her father at work and well-trained by him. The older sisters also could do so much more to satisfy the father and win his approval. So it came about that she regarded herself as hopeless, an outsider, inferior, ignored. In addition to all this she despised herself as feminine, which she could do nothing to change, save in imagination. The result of all this was that she set up barriers, made herself hard, adopted a pose of not caring, and froze herself and became petrified.

However, underneath all this hard façade there was a deep longing to be loved and to give love. She could be most sympathetic and generous, as she said, 'If I could do something for love I should be alright.' But within the home there was little opportunity for the expression of love, for the children were paid for everything they did, which was deeply resented in that it appeared that they were not allowed to love. Everything was on a strict business basis of 'x' work and 'x' pay. As herself she was not allowed to exist, and she remarked, 'I was treated as a machine.' She said she often felt there to be a kind of sack over her head, and of this she would dream. Her unconscious was showing her how her most distinctive and unique part of her Self, her face, was not being seen; she was but a sack and a pair of hands.

I will end this part of her story by relating a dream :

'I came to St Margaret's for my treatment, and I entered the room and saw an empty liqueur glass. You told me that you had been entertaining a famous golfer. You half-heartedly said you thought you might be able to fit me in on Friday afternoon. I was furious. As I was leaving I met my friend Ruth Jones at the front-door, and we had a conversation together about the shabby treatment, which was in a whisper because Mrs Ducker might hear us, for she was being most pleasant to two boys in the hall. As we walked up Church Gate some boys said, "Hello, Ruth !" She was cross with them for so addressing her, and she said, "Jones". When we came to the Clock Tower we looked in a shop window where children's clothes were displayed.'

I represented her father, my wife her mother. Her father had been giving preferential treatment to a famous golfer, that is, to one of her big brothers. She was furious towards her father for favouring the boys, and who measured out his affection according to achievement. Her mother was talking affectionately to two boys, who were her two younger brothers. She was outside the door, while they were inside, which made her very angry. Moreover, the father, who thought that 'he might be able to fit her in on Friday afternoon,' had adopted the attitude that anything left over (Friday afternoon) was good enough for her, whilst her mother cold-shouldered her, if for no other reason than that she had produced the two younger brothers. This was the point where she became cold and petrified. She had done what she could to give herself value by doing things, but this was useless. There will be noted resistance to the analyst, who was taking the projection of the bad images of the parents.

The dream then shows how she 'rode a high horse,' and turned part of herself into Ruth, a dignified and cultured person. The two urchins, again the two young brothers, came up to her and cheekily addressed her now dignified self with an 'Hello !' but immediately she added 'Jones'. This matter of a name was most important to her. She was fighting for her identity, and at the same time she was trying to impress her value upon the young brothers. The shop they came to, with the children's clothes in the window, reminded the dreamer of an occasion when her mother bought her two expensive frocks. These stood for her feminine value, and also for mother giving her love, that is value as a person. She had long tried to be helpful in the home in order to give herself value by her work, but when these actions were appreciated the approval went to what she had done rather than to herself as a person. What she wanted more than anything else in the world was to be of value in herself.

This feeling of having value comes to the child from outside himself, from the intimate world of relationships where the child is both seen and heard, and allowed to be both a giver and a receiver. It has, I hope, been made clear how important it is for the child to be loved regardless of his actions, although the opposite error must be avoided of giving the impression that deeds do not matter. There is a position between these two opposites. The importance of one emphasis has been stressed, that of establishing the child's sense of his individual value both by confirmation at many points in life, and also by distinguishing him from his actions. Actions, the good works of the New Testament, follow upon faith, and that faith is, in part at least, faith in oneself.

CHAPTER 5

PARENTAL INCONSISTENCIES

The effect of the character of the parent upon the child has long been recognized, and the importance of home life is a commonplace, but it is only recently that the intrapersonal relationship between the child and his parent has been deeply studied, and much research is being done. In this chapter I shall deal with the harmful effects of the various forms of parental inconsistency, the 'double-bind', and attributions. These do the gravest hurt to the child in that they divide his personality, they split it, and there can be nothing more disastrous and tragic than this breaking of the unity of the self, although, of course, there are degrees in which this takes place.

We must again emphasize the fact that the child develops through his relationships, and that he is not a self-contained unit. In a real sense he lives the lives of other people, and his health, or wholeness, is dependent upon the life of the community in which his life is set. Bearing this in mind try to imagine the effect of inconsistencies in the parents upon the development of the child, particularly those in the mother to whom the infant is so closely attached. The mother at first *is* the external world, and therefore when that mother-world is in a state of flux the infant will suffer the maximum confusion.

Confusion is one of the worst enemies of the child, for when he is confused he cannot establish his personal identity. He grows up through the identification he makes with people other than his mother, and he will share their lives. But if the life he then shares, which will naturally include that of his father and older brothers and sisters, is inconsistent the child will again fail to find a point of stability within himself. Life is now one thing, now another, and in vain will he try to bring together the opposite ends of himself. Or it may be that when he attempts to be two or more irreconcilable persons, as when he tries to identify himself with two irreconcilable parents. In despair he may give it all up as a bad job and make himself someone other than his real self, no matter how disastrous this course may be. This is the way out into delusion. On the other hand he may feel addled, directionless, stifled and stultified.

It has been maintained that alternations in the mother's attitude towards the infant are at least in part responsible for the fluctuating moods of the manic depressives. These are people who can be at one moment in the depths of despair and the next be on the top of the world gleefully distributing 'fivers', if they have them, to all and sundry. I have often been told by parents of the moodiness of their parents, as, for example, the case of the father who would go into a mood for weeks and only speak to the mother through the child. This child was forced to live in a divided world which most seriously split her personality.

Sometimes the inconsistency is due to conflicting parental images, as in the case of a young man who, as a child, was erotically stimulated by his very sentimental mother, and at the same time the feelings were condemned out of hand by the attitude of his grandmother, his other mother. The two mother images in his mind conflicted, and stimulation and condemnation synchronizing put the child into a state of unbearable confusion. This is one of the modes listed by H. F. Searles[1] by which a person is driven crazy. In this particular instance two of the six modes he gives are involved. The first is, as we have just seen, the combination or alternation of stimulation and frustration, and the other is the placing of a person in a position where there is sexual stimulation in a situation where it would be disastrous to have it gratified. Perhaps a third of Searles' modes was operative in this case for the young man was brought up in a strong moral environment. He would see himself as a definite type of character and the mother's attitude would stimulate in him an area of himself which he did not recognize. This situation is given the first place in H. F. Searles' list. You will note in these instances how the developing infant is split within himself, and in a way which will make him so confused that he cannot make head or tail of life.

The fourth mode indicated is illustrated by the young man I mentioned previously, who was brought up to measure everything rationally.[2] Reasoning was the only calculus he was trained to use, and since he was an infant prodigy in intelligence he could work out this rational mode of assessment at a remarkably early age. His emotional side had no chance to develop, and it was reduced to the barest minimum, and despised at that. Although he was unable to escape from emotion altogether, it was completely unrelated to the other level of his experience, and thus he was split.

Searles' fifth mode is the confusing difference of evaluation of an emotional situation. A particular thing is now felt to be good, now bad; now serious, now funny. Under these circumstances how can the child make value judgments? The child's reactions to the good

---

[1] "The effort to drive the other person crazy. . ." *Brit. J. Med. Psychol.* 32, 1. (Quoted by Laing).
[2] p. 49.

or bad, the serious or the funny, will be tossed like a shuttlecock, and this obviously comes under the heading of parental inconsistency. We can begin to understand the basic instability of a child subjected to these fluctuations, and his incapacity to make standard valuations in life.

The sixth mode is seen in the mixing up very divergent topics with one state of feeling. For example, the one emotional level is maintained whilst discussing the sublime and the ridiculous, the serious and the trivial, so that again the infant is unable to relate himself in any true sense to the world of values. He will be at a loss to know how to sift the wheat from the chaff, and he will be in a permanent state of confusion and inability to cope with life.

It may be found by the child that the parent does not remain consistent with his own injunctions, as when he teaches honesty and is dishonest himself. A certain young man was given the most puritanical rules regarding sex by his father, yet his father went off with a barmaid! Such inconsistencies can only result in serious psychological conflict for the child, and may even create an inner state of confusion. Amid the chaos of such upbringing the child is unable to attain a clear sense of direction.

A similar confusion must arise when the parents and children split between themselves, as in the case of two sons, one of whom was the apple of his father's eye, and the other of the mother's. It was as though one boy was motherless and the other fatherless, each one of them being disowned by a parent. The result was that everything they did was pleasing to one parent, and displeasing to the other.

There must be some confusion when the parents themselves set different standards, as when mother goes to church and the father does not, or when mother is a staunch Protestant and the father is a practising Roman Catholic. In many cases the conflict will be resolved by the child taking one side, but this will put him in an emotional opposition to the other parent. Although this kind of inconsistency is not as serious as some, yet it hurts the child, especially when the parents will not 'live and let live' in their attitudes towards one another, and the result is that it becomes more difficult for the child to adjust himself to reality.

The home should not be so 'unified' as to be too narrow for the development of individuality. There must be healthy oppositions which are held good naturedly, so that the child can develop without undue emotional tension. In fact there are bound to be found various constitutional differences amongst the members of the family which enrich the environment. However, when the parents are of opposite temperaments, or when their constitutions are different from that of the child trouble easily arises, as Dr Anthony Storr has pointed out in his book, *The Integrity of the Personality*.[1]

Geoffrey, whom I have mentioned earlier,[2] was completely dominated by his grandmother, as was his highly emotional and timid mother. When the father came home from active service he exercised his authority, and we can readily visualize how the scene was set for considerable confusion and inconsistency in the child's home. One mother laid down the law and saw it enforced, the other mother was weak and vacillating, and these feminine variations utterly confused the child. Further, their standards were chaotic, for one moment a thing was right, the next it was wrong. 'Children should not sit,' the grandmother said, 'they should be running about,' but as soon as he got up he was roundly reprimanded for not keeping still. If he were noisy he should be quiet, but when he was quiet he was asked what was wrong with him!

The women were dominant, particularly since the father was away from home, but when he returned a new disruptive element entered the child's life which he could not understand. Besides this, the father was himself a moody person, as Geoffrey said, 'he blew hot and cold, I never knew whether he was going to kick or kiss me.' There were occasions when his father would say how proud he was of his son, and at other times he would ignore or threaten him. One day he bought the boy a toy gramophone with a record called 'My Kid', which was a song of a proud father to his small boy. We can appreciate how Geoffrey would love to hear that record, which he would interpret as his father's voice expressing his pride in him. But the father driven to distraction by the endless tune and words, which may well have upset his guilt complex, shouted, 'If you play that thing again I will smash it up.' The child simply could not believe it. There were two voices: the one acclaimed him, whilst the other threatened the destruction of his precious toy.

He said his father was one moment absurdly generous and at another extremely niggardly, for example, he would take him on long train journeys to see football matches and on one occasion bought him a fine bicycle. In later life he would clear away the snow from the drive so that Geoffrey could take out the car and go to a dance, and then, at other times, he would show him no consideration whatever, and would seem completely disinterested.

It is interesting that Geoffrey recalls trying to work out the meaning of these fluctuations, and he would ask himself, 'What have I

[1] p. 62.
[2] p. 35.

done to cause these changes?' As is typical of children, he did not see anything wrong in his parents, and argued within himself that whatever wrong there was must be in him. Even to this day his head whirls with confusion, and he still asks, 'What sort of a world is this?' We can see that it was impossible for the child to develop into healthy manhood and obtain secure bearings in a topsy-turvy world like that. Every day would appear more complicated than the one before, until the summation of complexity and confusion became unbearable.

Such inconsistency inevitably breeds fear and insecurity in the child, and the spirit of venture and trust is frustrated 'ab initio'. What is left to such a child but to withdraw from a world so full of difficulties? His most precious coinage was his love, and when he gave this sometimes it was accepted, at others it was completely ignored, and at other times it even brought punishment upon him. A child then can do nothing with love but love himself, and gain whatever satisfaction he can within his own inner world. It is by no means surprising that today, in middle-age, Geoffrey lives in a world of fantasy.

I have written before[1] about another aspect of parental inconsistency under the heading of 'The Harmful Effects of Parental Disharmony'. When the father, mother and child do not stand together in a unity at a certain level, that is when they do not essentially consist, the framework of the personality is damaged. It is bad enough to face the breakdown in parental relationships in later life, but it is a most shattering and confusing thing when the child is very young. I have often found this to be a serious cause of splitting in the personality. The masculine and the feminine components, which are the two basic aspects of the Self, are prevented from coming together to form a whole Self. The infant may remain in a permanent state of confusion, or he may try to work himself out of the dilemma by taking one side or the other. In this latter case he may go over into a homosexual position as he sides with his father, or he may feel that he has no masculinity with which to confront the feminine which dominates his life. The latter may drive him into considerable trouble through envy of his father. These inner states of confusion and unbalance are reflected in the person's total response to his environment. An alternative reaction is that of the hysteric who oscillates between his parents, now clinging to one, now to the other; or who adopts a 'running with the hare and a hunting with the hounds' attitude.

A severely dissociated hysteric who came to me for help was much occupied with stereophonic recording of music. He always felt 'high

---

[1] *A Christian Therapy for a Neurotic World*, p. 108.

fidelity' had a psychological significance for him, and he related this to his parents. The stereophonic effect was a symbolic attempt to hear his parents as a unity. At a later time his interest switched to stereoscopic vision, and whilst in this phase he had much trouble with his eyes and he was given glasses by his optician. He purchased the most expensive type of binoculars on the market, which again he felt to have an inner significance. Finally he realized that this was but another attempt to see his parents as a unity.

'The Double-bind'

There are some situations in which the child is wrong whatever he may do. These are known as 'the double-bind', and they have been investigated by the American psychologist Bateson. The child is sincere and he is criticized, therefore he adopts the pattern he believes his parents want him to follow, and then they say he is not being true. Either way he is wrong, and there is nothing to be done about it. Thackeray's young man in *Pendennis* was told that he must adopt a way of life other than his own, but when he did he was denounced. Continued exposure to this kind of thing can have very serious results.

A girl who was brought up in a very genteel and scholastic home was faced with such a dilemma, for her dominant mother decided just what her daughter should be like. She must be polite and well behaved, she must be a thoroughbred lady. When she behaved in accordance with this pattern she was wrong, because her mother also insisted that she should stand up for herself. When she expressed herself freely then she was not being polite and socially acceptable, and therefore again in the wrong; she was expected to be two incompatible beings.

A common instance of the principle behind the double-bind is to be found in the kitchen. The child is expected to come to mother to find her love and care, so he gives his love to her, and runs to her. Unfortunately she is in the middle of a hazardous cooking operation, and so she not only sends him away, but looks and sounds cross. All the child knows is that if he does not love mother he is ever insecure and lost, but when he does love her he is also lost, for she is cross and sends him away from her. Thus whatever he does is wrong and disastrous. Parents whose emotional life is unnaturally bound up with their children are likely to perpetuate the double-bind. They call the child out to themselves, whilst their own hidden guilt prevents the fulfilment of the act as it were mid-stream. Then there is a 'You must' and a 'You must not' at the same moment.

There is a further complication in these situations which comes from the old enemy, fear. Could the child escape from the dilemma of the two opposing demands by just escaping from the situation in which they arose, he could shake the dust from off his feet and be little the worse for it. This, however, is the very last thing he can do, because his fear of separation binds him to the mother, or whoever it is. If the thought of escape crossed his mind the next moment he would realize the sheer impossibility of living without the loved object upon whom he is so dependent.

The girl I mentioned in Chapter 4, whose father was so great a worker, suffered from this kind of problem. There was a very strong family sense, so strong that it came between the individual member of the family and his freedom. Again, the parents, quite unconsciously, were possessive of their children, and at times they would not hesitate to remind them how much they had done for them. It was hinted that they should look after them in old age. I have already mentioned the way in which the duty to work bound all of them as with the tentacles of an octopus. In three ways the children were smothered: by the family, by the parents, and by work. In order to be an individual self the girl felt she must break away from these three binds, and to achieve this she left home believing it would break the bond, but without effect, for she was bound emotionally to this unconscious system. The bane of it was that she could not permit herself to be free, for freedom meant disloyalty to the family, ingratitude to the parents, and neglect of duty, which was work. And yet, conflicting with all this, was loyalty to herself as a person and duty towards herself an an individual being. The one ruled out the other, and yet she could not live without both.

Another person, feeling herself morally bound to her parents, also felt herself bound to society in which her fuller life lay. But if she sided with her parents she felt all wrong with society, and if she sided with society she was all wrong with her parents. Both were deemed to be essential to her. Whatever she did was wrong, and there was no alternative or compromise possible.

Someone else felt her family to be like a vacuum cleaner sucking her into it. To do as she was expected to do completely emptied her, but likewise she would be destroyed if she broke away from her family, for she simply could not live apart from her family.

The Parable of the Prodigal Son (St Luke XV) may be used to illustrate a particular form of this problem. We may safely assume that the son's home was above average in respect of its standards of behaviour. The father showed forth an extraordinary ability for creativity and progressiveness in that he allowed his son to leave home at will, never once preventing him from taking his venture into the outside world. Again, when the son had left the family, the father demonstrated his willingness for the son's return by running out to meet him. The son was really accepted back into the fold, and was given the place of honour instead of being despised for having 'run away'.

Even so, the son had to wrestle with a deep personal problem within himself. He had realized that to remain in the confines of his family meant being fettered to an infinite demand for all-protecting and all-providing parents. It is only natural for parents to want children to be as good as they think they are themselves, and this feeling is all too easily conveyed to the children. The demands that are imposed upon the child in this way are in fact too great, for the youngsters should be absorbed in the processes of their own individuation. But instead of being allowed to develop along their own lines, and to find their own identities, the children are all too often side-tracked and are led along other channels of development. Parents will often teach their children to be what they are not, i.e. 'good', 'well-mannered', and perhaps above all 'reasonable'. This is an unconscious process, and I feel sure that it is handed down from generation to generation. The elder brother in the parable was one of those sweet-tempered children, he could never understand the motives for his young brother's departure. 'Fancy leaving us like that, deserting us. How unreasonable of him!'

As the Bible story tells us, he was deeply hurt to find that his brother had gained a reward on his return. This elder brother was never to know the joy of a safe homecoming from a venture into the perils and perplexities of everyday life. He was gutless. He always clung to the shelter that his family afforded: but in that shelter there was no room to move and express himself. He always kept an eye cocked on himself lest he should be swallowed up in the darkness of disapproval. Jung taught us that we must face the darkness, the shadow side of our personalities, neither bargaining with it nor making any form of compromise. In most people the difficulty is created not by any problem of the moment, but in the making of an escape from a situation that was intolerable in years past.

The more these people run away, the more terrifying the age-old threat seems. A bind is created from which there seems no escape at all. By running away they only increase the pressure upon themselves, and this is promoted by their fear of being found wanting should the demands of another crisis be forced upon them.

Once they can lay themselves open to attack they will find that they are no longer plagued by the *threat* of attack. The old saying which states, 'Once bitten, twice shy' might serve as a reminder that it is not the bite which works the emotional havoc, but the shying away from the essential crisis.

The only safety for the chicks seems to be under the feathers of the hen, but the feathers present destructive smothering, the stifling negation of every impulse. Everything is wrong and threatening. Confusion reigns supreme, the child can neither fight—for fear of destroying that which is vital to his needs, nor can he flee—for separation is quite intolerable. The result seems to be that the child is left in a vacuum, a very uncomfortable state of suspension between two opposing poles which are bringing seemingly crippling pressures to bear upon him. In this situation there seems to be no escape at all, and all the time fear mounts inside the child. This element of fear is just the very thing that binds the child tighter and tighter upon himself.

Another aspect of the double-bind may be found in the child's need to feel thought of by his parents, for when being thus in the thoughts of his parents he feels that he belongs to them and has significance. Even to be thought of in a bad way is better than not to be thought of at all. But if one cannot live without being thought of, it is possible to be thought of in such a way that it destroys life, hence the double-bind. Parents can so hold the child in their minds that he feels himself to be possessed by them. He is so open to scrutiny that there is no corner of his soul he can call his own, he is so cared for that he despairs of himself as an individual being. In the scrutiny he is not confirmed as a Self, he is held, but not supported in his essential being. This 'care and thought' brings no vestige of freedom, no courage to go into the world and face life as a mature person. The 'care' is often parental worry concerning the child, which only frightens him, and makes him insecure, and therefore binds him in his dependence.

D. H. Lawrence said that it is the duty of parents ' "mentally" to forget but dynamically never to forsake their children.'[1] When this wise precept is followed there will be no fear of causing a double-bind. A patient of mine experienced the contrary, and of this he wrote, 'My parents were in this position of being unable to let go of me, because though good, God-fearing people they were prevented from having any idea of what "never dynamically forsaking" could mean, and this I think because, although they were "religious", they had no sense of wonder in life. All life's problems and opportunities had to be approached with utmost circumspection.' His story would have been very different had his parents digested the lines from 'The Prophet' by Kahlil Gibran :

[1] *Fantasia of the Unconscious*, p. 126—American ed.

'Your children are not your children.
They are the sons and daughters of Life's longing for itself.
They come through you, but not from you
And though they with you, yet they belong not to you.
You may give them your love but not your thoughts
For they have their own thoughts.
You may house their bodies but not their souls,
For their souls dwell in the house of tomorrow
Which you cannot visit, not even in your dreams.
You may strive to like them.
But seek not to make them like you
For life goes not backward nor tarries with yesterday.
You are the bows from which your children as living arrows are sent
forth.
The Archer sees the mark upon the path of the infinite
And He bends you with His might that His arrows may go swift and far.
Let your bending to the Archer's hand be for gladness,
For even as He loves the arrow that flies
So He loves also the bow that is stable.'

It was the destructive nature of the binding, of which we have been thinking, which led Lawrence to inveigh so much against the excessive stressing of the understanding and the will in Western civilization. He felt humanity was being poisoned by understanding in that it was killing the deep roots of life which lie in our bodies. This understanding, he maintained, makes slaves of people, lays them open to dissection and incises the essential mystery of life. Jung wrote 'Nothing is more unbearable for the patient than to be always understood,'[1] which is a dictum the analyst should never forget, for in so doing he will perpetuate the error of the parents who destroy the child by means of all-pervading understanding. It is this 'understanding' of man which gives rise to such criticism of psychology as is expressed by G. A. Studdert-Kennedy; who himself was knowledgeable of psychology:

'He takes the saint to pieces,
And labels all the parts,
He tabulates the secrets
Of loyal loving hearts.
He probes their selfless passion,
And shows exactly why
The martyr goes out singing,
To suffer and to die.
The beatific vision
That brings them to their knees

[1] *Modern Man in Search of a Soul*, p. 10 (Routledge paperback).

> He smilingly reduces
> To infant fantasies . . .
> His reasoning is perfect
> His proofs as plain as paint,
> He has but one small weakness,
> He cannot make a saint.'[1]

Thus Lawrence saw the 'do-gooders' and the 'humanists', who understand man, as ego-centrics who undo man by their understanding of him. We would add the names of many parents who undo their children by this very means.

Only those, I think, who are religious can appreciate the meaning of dynamically never forsaking, because it seems to me to involve men in a purpose beyond the purely personal: as Lawrence asked, 'Is there nothing beyond my fellow man? If not, then there is nothing beyond myself . . . my neighbour is but myself in a mirror. So we toil in a circle of pure egoism.'

The child caught up in the double-bind is in a truly desperate position, and as an analogy, one might consider a wasp inside a jam-jar, making every effort to gain a hold of the invisible glass, but succeeding only in digging into the imprisoning jam, to its complete despair and ultimate destruction of either:

a. being himself, and losing his relationship with his parents, or
b. maintaining his relationship with his parents but failing to become a true self.

The thing that is so elusive about the problem is that neither the sufferer, nor those around him, understand what is going on within themselves and between themselves, and in the terms of the analogy this reflects the invisible nature of the glass. The child will know instinctively that 'something is wrong', but he can get no further without help from outside the imprisoning family circle. As Dr Graham Howe points out, the situation is knitted so unconsciously by the parents, and the 'negative atmosphere' is wrought with such good intention that it stands as an invisible quicksand into which all may fall quite obliviously.

Attributions

Dr R. D. Laing has described in his book *The Self and Others* the adverse effects of Attributions. These are the attributes that are ascribed to a young person, against which he has no court of appeal, no means by which he can deny the validity of what is being attributed to him. Geoffrey, whom I mentioned earlier, was told as a child

---

[1] "The Psychologist" from *The Unutterable Beauty*.

that he was no good, and this became a family saying. It was doubt-less said as a joke, but it was no joke to the child, who accepted the attribution literally. Another small boy was told that he would never make a man, and the attribution could not be disproved. As Dr Laing says, such statements seem to have global significance. The child may be so discouraged that he tells himself that it is no good trying to be good, or a significant person at all, and he then may take the path to utter irresponsibility. On the other hand the attribution may be of an angelic order—'You're a perfect angel,' 'You're a saint if there ever was one,' 'someday you will be a Bishop or the Prime Minister. . . .' Repeatedly hearing such attributions the child may well grow up into a prig, the smug self-righteous Pharisee, or a thoroughly disillusioned and bitter person.

Another kind of attribution is that of the parent or teacher who imposes his ideas upon the child with such authority that the child introjects them into himself, and he becomes indoctrinated. For ex-ample, a young man told me how his mother has shaped his life in this way. This was how he reported the matter:

'Mother said, "I don't like music, so you don't.
        I don't like soup, so you don't.
        I don't like bicycles, so you don't.
        I don't like holidays, so you don't.
        I don't like reading, so you don't.
        I don't like having friends, so you don't." '

There were a few positive versions of this, such as:
        'I like medicine, so you must.
        I like work, so you must.'

Another instance of this kind of thing was seen in the boy who was told day by day 'You've got to be careful,' and just what this meant was undefined. At other times he was told 'You're very steady . . . you're very patient,' and although many a time he felt furious within, eventually he was effectively brain-washed, and became meek and mild. Again he was told, 'Your muscles are softer than those of other lads,' and the insidious implication did its work and he came to believe that on various scores he was altogether inferior and weaker than other boys. A similar instance of this was found in the little girl whose mother repeatedly told her she was not like other children, because she had her own individuality and did not do what many other chil-dren do, but in the end the force of the attribution was irresistible and she came to regard herself as peculiar, to her great hurt.

Thus these three, parental inconsistency, the double-bind, and attributions, inflict deep hurt upon the child. Loyalty to himself is made to conflict with loyalty to others, the child is basically confused, he is placed in a life situation in which whatever he does he is 'destroyed', and his life is compelled to become a living lie for the reason that he is made to be what he is not. These are ways in which the integrity of a person is destroyed and individual identity is lost. It is no exaggeration to say that this is criminal activity on the part of parents and teachers, the tragic part of it is that it is often done with the best intentions, and that the 'best' parents are most likely to do this kind of thing.

The end of the story is not in the direct result of this adverse activity, but it is in the reactions which the child is led to make. He may well try to cover up the hurt which is being done, or has been done, by pretences, two-facedness, secrecy in which he outwardly complies with his authorities and at the same time seeks his own ends, and repressions which work their own evil work ever after. Whatever the child does he cannot escape the tragic fact that he has been split within his personality, and that in a real way he does not know his name.

CHAPTER 6

SELF-PUNISHMENT

'. . . then thou shalt give life for life, eye for eye, tooth for tooth, hand for hand, foot for foot, burning for burning, wound for wound, stripe for stripe.' *(Exodus XXI, 23–25.)*

This Lex Talionis is something wider in experience than the Jewish law, for it is engraved upon the soul of man. A moment's reflection reveals it to us by way of a sense of elementary justice, for what we give out, we feel, we must receive back, whether it be good or evil. When we do good we expect it to be duly noted somewhere, and we have an expectation that the good should return to us in some shape or form, in other words we expect goodness to be rewarded. But when it does not come back to us we find ourselves warming to a sense of grievance, which may soon become a consuming sense of injustice, or if not this, we may find ourselves wrapped in self-pity. 'I have not deserved this considering all I have done!' and 'The wrongs against me cry out to high heaven! Why should I work, put myself out, or even love, considering what I have given to others?' These, and such like cries, are commonplace, and they are founded upon the assumption that what we receive shall be related to what we have given. On the other hand, if we have done evil then we must suffer an equal measure of evil, and if the law does not catch up on us we ourselves must impose upon ourselves a judgment which demands that we make acts of expiation; and in cases where this demand is unconscious the atonement may be made without ceasing.

Religion is concerned with this self-imposed canon of self-punishment. In the Old Testament times people were struggling against old retaliations and vendettas, but, even then, as we know, it was possible for a man to administer unjust judgments in the Name of God. However, there is another voice beginning to be heard, which proclaims that God and God alone is Judge. He sided with Cain against the natural desire to hunt down the criminal and punish him, and in this He was taking the matter of punishment, in important respects, out of man's hands.

It is in the New Testament, however, that a new authoritative voice is heard, saying, 'But I say unto you, Love your enemies.' And this is something we have to learn to do with the great enemy within ourselves, our guilt, which is for ever demanding of us merciless self-punishment. There is an aspect of the Cross which has utmost relevance to such a situation, in which we see Christ carrying our guilt and shame for us. For that end He died. In conscious life the knowledge of this is as clear as the day, but all too often the guilt-laden person still continues to punish himself, as though 'the price for sin' had not been paid. The explanation for this lies in the fact that the unconscious is incapable of assimilating the Good News, and consciousness is powerless to effect this deep and essential change. It is here where we see illustrated the great help psychotherapy can give for in the vast majority of cases only its special techniques can penetrate this hidden and controlling realm. When this exercise is completed one of the worst scourges in the experience of man is removed, remorseless self-punishment. It is a far more fearful thing to fall into the hands of man than of God, but even fellow man could not be so sadistic as we often are with ourselves (masochism).

A patient of mine was truly fascinated by fantasy in which he saw himself lying half-naked on the altar step, where a huge man with a terrible whip was scourging him. He himself was both those men. He was flaying himself for God to see, in the hope that God, witnessing his self-punishment, would forgive him.

Another patient saw himself in a dream in which he was mutilating himself most horribly with a razor, after which he would never be any good in life. Following upon this was a second nightmare in which a man was chasing him with a gun, and here again, the chaser, and would-be destroyer, was no other than himself. This dream ended by the man holding, on either side of his head, two bombs which he was going to explode. He was a weak and feeble little man in appearance, unhealthily placid, dominated by his mother and sister. By means of his self-punishment he had deprived himself of marriage and a home of his own, and latterly he had deprived himself of his capacity for work. He had not been free from a headache for many months, and this ensured that he could not enjoy himself in any way! And now he was submitting himself to the supreme punishment.

Physical symptoms are common forms of self-punishment. The man I mentioned, who was prostrate on the altar step in his dream, unconsciously punished himself with fibrositis which disturbed his sleep for several weeks, and when that began to subside he developed a most irritating rash. Such self-made Jobs are far more numerous than we realize, though I am not suggesting for a moment that all fibrositis and every rash has this kind of causation. I have written elsewhere[1]

[1] A *Christian Therapy for a Neurotic World*, pp. 142, 175 (the same person).

of people who, through similar unconscious motivations, are prone to accidents.

When the hysteric puts on his acts to impress the world, or to bring himself love and sympathy by evoking pity, there is something within him which knows he is acting a lie. He feels he is being dishonest with life, and this sense of dishonesty itself creates further guilt for which he has to punish himself still more. Thus the symptoms produced to evoke pity are at the same time his instruments of self-punishment, and we need to understand that he cannot surrender this self-punishment, for then he would have to face the full weight of unexpiated guilt. So long as he suffers his symptoms, or the neurotic illness itself, he can remain unconscious of the guilt.

It is not difficult to understand the serious hurt done to such guilt-ridden persons as we are considering by telling them what wicked people they are. Often this hurt is caused in the name of religion, but it is not only religion which makes an already intolerable burden more intolerable. The courts, in a far more public way than religion ever does, can bind on people crimes which in fact they have not committed. A young schizophrenic I know was told in court that consideration was being given to his being sent to prison, but the young man himself was scarcely aware of having committed the crime for which he was being punished, for he was grievously mentally sick. Doubtless the intention of the Judge was to make a salutary impression upon the offender for his good, but such treatment of a person already thrashing himself within an inch of his life is not merely clumsy and inexcusable, it is downright cruelty.

We need not look to religion and the law alone for this kind of thing. The mother of a very ill patient of mine definitely set about to inculcate a sense of guilt in her small son, for this was her method of upbringing. She was always critical of him, and on principle she never praised him, instead she insisted he could never do a single thing right. She would run him down in front of his friends when they came to tea, and that in no uncertain way, at times even going to the extent of swearing at him. It is obvious that the mother was a very sick person herself, and this was borne out by the fact that when her husband tried to take a strong line with her she would fall on the floor and roll about, which is a sure sign of guilt. You will recall people throwing themselves on the ground in the Bible, and in so doing they were expressing their guilt. The mother was projecting her own guilt on to her son. On the occasions when the father did not have his own way, the mother insisted that he punished the boy; fortunately the boy knew perfectly well that his father was only pretending to punish him, which made him feel that he had an ally in his father. The mother's authority was her power to make the child feel guilty, and it is no wonder that the son came to me in a very sick condition. In almost every drawing he brings to his sessions there is a Cross, but it is his own cross, and it is the measure of his self-punishment. He is crucifying himself, for he came to accept his mother's valuation of himself, that is, he accepted her attribution.

This is, I agree, an extreme case of induced guilt, but there are many parents who less violently, though effectively, rule their young by making them bear guilt. Their sick and distorted consciences, which have to be broken down in analysis, bear ample testimony to this.

The sharp edge to guilt may be the dis-confirmation it carries. The guilty feel outcast, rejected, despised, 'a scorn and derision.' Such words describe our Lord on the Cross Who was bearing our guilt. To be rejected is to feel bad, as an apple is bad. Infants who feel no loving response is being made to their love immediately jump to the conclusion that they are utterly worthless, that no matter what they do there is no way back into life, for their total activity is woefully tainted by an inner rottenness. To this feeling of rottenness they attach their guilt. Some poor people are so overwhelmed by their appalling sense of guilt that they become melancholics, and may be seen on their knees, wringing their hands, and beseeching God for mercy which never comes to them. Such people are racked by misery and remorse to an infinite degree, and their disorders always have their deepest roots in babyhood. When the loss of love appears to be final there is an experience of final rejection and the annihilation of hope, and then only blank and utter despair remains. Guilt is the most terrible thing, and we must be watchful lest in zeal for righteousness we unwittingly do the Devil's work.

The grandmother of another patient of mine did this Devil's work most effectively. This man, in his early forties, came from a professional background and a good Christian home. His parents were kind and helpful and models of what a man and wife should be. But in the background lurked the grandmother, who lived with the family, and she was very possessive of her grandchild, and also a veritable expert on Hell Fire. Unknown to his parents she exerted a tremendous negative influence upon the child, which reached its climax, when the child was about three years of age, when she caught the small child masturbating, as all children are inclined to do. The old dear thought she was doing God's work in terrifying the child about his natural self, and she succeeded all too well, for she inspired him with a sense of utmost guilt and shame. To quote, 'She indoctrinated into me a belief that I was a great sinner, that God would damn me, that

I would be an outcast in this world, being viewed with contempt and sent to Coventry, and that in the next world I would be destined to everlasting punishment if I persisted in my habits. She said that the Devil had put sexual desires into me and that I would lose my soul. She told me that everyone who met me would automatically despise me. I remember coming down in the morning wishing to assume the role of a girl rather than a boy. At a later age of ten years, somebody told me something about kissing girls under the mistletoe and I was filled with shame in consequence of my great guilt. Similarly whenever I saw a seedy or knock-kneed child, I imagined this was due to a sin similar to mine, from which I had been narrowly saved. At the age of thirty I still loathed to be seen speaking to a young woman, and I blushed with shame, if anyone teased me on the subject.'

'I went at the age of eight to a private school where I met with very hostile treatment from the other children. One child stamped on my feet, but I never mentioned the incident to anyone, as I believed I deserved what I got.'

Later he went to another school where he was regarded as an oddity and life was most unpleasant. The headmaster was brutal and tyrannical and his favourite phrase was, 'You can't hit a boy too hard!' To continue his story, he said:

'My attitude was that I must always be wrong. I operated from the angle that I must be no good. I was bad, and therefore I must bow to everyone else, because they were better than I. If anyone said a nasty thing there must be some truth in it, and I therefore had no answer to it. 'Fear, not freedom, ruled my life. I could not accept responsibility because I lacked freedom to operate for myself. I believed my value lay in doing all I could to conform. I believed I could never be valued for being myself. If I were rebuked or punished, I punished myself tenfold, and was full of guilt.'

Later he went to Oxford where he was nervous, self-conscious, and lacking in confidence. On leaving the university he passed into the army where the tension mounted to such a degree that he was finally discharged with a nervous breakdown. He was now in a thoroughly confused state, desperate about marriage, depressed, disinterested, weary and worried. He could find no place in life because he was overwhelmed by the idea that he was not a proper man. His rage, which he felt unable to express by means of manly aggressiveness, intensified and was turned inwards upon himself. Thus he presented a sorry picture of depression and morbid self-pity.

Behind this sad story of wasted life was severe guilt and constant self-punishment. He could not, like a man, defend himself, for the reason that his debility was the very medicine he had to take. He must stand up and allow himself to be hit. He punished himself by crediting himself with being a worm and no man, and by the adoption of a feminine position; further, he punished himself by the uncritical acceptance of all criticism of himself. There were also several disorders of a physical nature which fitted into the pattern of self-punishment.

We may be able to understand something of why certain people want to end life when hope has died and life has lost its significance, for there is then no point in struggling on with difficulties and bearing endless hardships. Such people seem to be making the ascent of Calvary Hill, and the descent into Hell, of which the Creed speaks, without any sense of purpose or achievement, and certainly without the assurance of the final victory of Easter. More often suicide is seen unconsciously as the supreme self-punishment. This step is taken because the burden of guilt has become intolerable, and there is seen to be no way of coping with it otherwise, nor any escape from it. When this attitude is broken down it may be found that the act was the final and complete atonement for guilt. It may also be punishment in anticipation, on the principle that 'I had better hurt myself than hurt someone else.' On the other hand, I have often listened to the cry, which comes from over the years, 'I wish I were dead.' These cries are born of excessive pressures and demands, complete lack of confirmation and encouragement, the intolerable sense of aloneness and disapproval.

Geoffrey,[1] whom I mentioned several times, had suicidal urges. He felt he could easily jump from his high office window, which draws him like a magnet. He spoke of suicide as something entirely reasonable, and thus he rationalized his need for self-punishment. Further, he was critical of the 'canon against self-slaughter' for he had set himself upon the throne of God and felt free to alter the Divine laws as he chose. For this reason he remarked that the idea that life is a gift from God is just 'utter phooey'. This same man pictured himself in a grocer's shop, and instead of cutting up the bacon he saw himself cutting off his fingers; at other times in his fantasy he would be a butcher chopping off his fingers one by one.

When people feel the need to make atonement it is, in many cases, an atonement for crimes which have only been committed in fantasy and are far removed from consciousness. Such people would in fact never have committed murder or any other aggressive or sexual crime, yet they are completely at the mercy of their fantastic underworld.

[1] E.g. p. 35.

Very often the people who suffer the most are the meek and mild, sensitive folk, and their self-inflicted punishments must hurt them quite beyond description. The deep fantasy crimes spring from baby rages, and later from numerous occasions of envy and jealously in infancy, from which the guilt persists down the years, and the expiatory suffering is never deemed adequate to settle the account. The only cure from the human standpoint is to trace the origins of the guilt in the unconscious, though some happy people may be able to break through the guilt by a deep experience of the love of God and of His atoning work upon the Cross. However, it must be emphasized that the inability to experience this demonstrates no lack of faith, but only a lack of capacity to feel deeply, which in itself is a symptom of psychological or emotional disorder. A feeling of lack of love would doubtless have caused the evil fantasies to arise, and therefore love freely given, and given without measure, heals the scars which the state of lovelessness created. But, may I say again in emphasis, all too often the sick person is just incapable, by the nature of his disorder, of experiencing this incoming love. Doors have been shut tightly against it, and at times love itself is felt to be the destroying thing for it draws us out of ourselves, and when there is felt to be far too little of the Self such out-going is seen as an absolute emptying of the Self. It is obvious, then, that people in this state cannot use the great gift of Divine Love if it makes any demand upon them, and love always does this in that it creates gratitude.

Masochistic pleasure is difficult to deal with, for it provides great relief from guilt, so that when a person gives up this pleasure he is faced with the full hurt of his guilt. As long as he punished himself, however much such punishment may hurt, he feels better for it, and this binds his self-punishments upon him.

Occasionally people produce dreams in which 'a child is being beaten.' Freud and Stekel have something to say about these dreams. Stekel,[1] amongst other things, related such dreams to homosexuality, and I mention this because a young man who came to see me, had such a dream, and was worried about his homosexual tendencies. Only certain boys attracted him, and these were what he described as 'sexual boys', and he felt himself to be drawn to them because he felt, at least unconsciously, that they could supply something that was lacking in himself, since he regarded himself to be less than a man. What they could contribute to him gave him a feeling of well-being and boosted his weak masculinity, and this, of course, made the exercise attractive to him. He was the boy in the dream, and pleasure

[1] *Sadism and Masochism*, Ch. IX and V.

would accrue to him by means of the beating on two accounts. First, he would receive a sexual stimulus, for physical hurt can be sexually stimulating; and secondly, the beating was punishment which would take away his sexual guilt. The fact that he felt he had to be punished for sexual desire dated back to the time when as a child he was punished on account of sex. The boys who affected him carried both his desire for sex, for you will remember they were 'sexual boys', and also his punishment for sex. He stated that his interest in boys was always tinged with sadism; the explanation of this lay in their carrying a projection of his own self-punishment, so that his desire to hurt them was his desire to hurt himself.

I have mentioned elsewhere the man who obtained pleasure from sticking needles in himself. He worked on the principle that he could only permit himself to enjoy pleasure after a corresponding amount of pain had been felt. This was prospective atonement, the paying of the bill before it had been sent in. I have met a number of people to whom Passiontide is a particularly painful time, for they see themselves as being crucified, and thereby making an atonement for their own guilt. The person who stuck himself with needles suffered as soon as Lent began, and it made him positively ill. He had a pleasure problem which produced a sexual perversion. He felt guilty if he enjoyed himself in any way, and he would be in agony afterwards for days, but never so much as when he permitted himself to have pleasure in Lent. He could not allow himself, although a Christian, to mention Christ's Name, nor could he allow himself to face a Cross. In his abject misery he said that if he could face the Cross he would be helped out of his misery, but he could not allow himself to do this, for he must go on suffering. He worked out his resistance to the Cross as being in part due to the sin of pride, as he said, 'If I could be rid of this pride I would be able to face the Cross and seek all the help it offers.' He had to carry the cross and be himself the victim, for he said, 'It is my cross, my hurt.' He had evolved his own system of salvation, for he would not allow anyone else to save him, and it was a system of salvation by works. He felt he must do good however distasteful it might be to him, in fact the more distasteful it was the more he liked it, for there was more self-punishment in it. He said, 'It is obvious that this necessary torment stood in the way of recovery, for without it he was bereft of his system of expiation.'

I also mentioned in my earlier book a young man who became ill in Holy Week and was taken to hospital. When he was coming round after his operation he asked, 'Is it Easter Day yet?' It was clear that he was treating his illness as an act of atonement, and Easter meant that the appointed time of suffering was over.

All these self-punishing people live lives of intense misery. They cannot allow themselves to be loved, and they cannot love themselves, and this is not because they have committed unforgiveable sins, but because they live in a world of unreality from which they cannot free themselves. The Church should be the first to recognize these grim states of mind, and she should be the first to come to the aid of those who suffer them, using the special insights and techniques, without which this service cannot be rendered, in the Name of her Lord.

CHAPTER 7

FANTASIES

It is a golden rule of psychotherapy that the patient himself must do the work, nevertheless he will not be alone in this for there is a 'spirit' within him which is guiding him all the time, the recognition of which is very important to the patient. His dreams and fantasies are the product of this inner spirit. It is one thing to be told a fact about oneself, but it is quite a different matter to dream about the fact, for it then carries a special kind of authority for the dreamer. Admittedly the dream may seem nonsense until it is interpreted, but the interpretation, when correct, carries conviction. If the interpretation is mistaken, or if something important to the work of individuation has been overlooked, the theme will be repeated in a later dream until the hitherto unconscious contents have been fully assimilated to the conscious outlook. It is as though the spirit within man will give him no peace until the problem is solved, until he has reached a certain measure of wholeness.

I have mentioned a young man who was an infant prodigy[1] and whose intellect left little room for anything else in his life. In the following story, in which he gave free rein to his imagination, he himself showed in no uncertain way what had happened to him.

'I was librarian in charge of a large public library. One morning, when I had been there for about three months, a girl came in and asked me if I would help her to find some books. She said, "I want the first lot for my boy friend," and she asked, "Have you *Andersen's Fairy Tales?* and *Grimms' Fairy Tales?* and I would be most grateful if you could find me a copy of the music of *Baa Baa Black Sheep.*" I did not pass any comment on the selection of the books required for her boy friend, but collected them as requested. Then she said, "Now I would like some also. Have you *Differential Calculus? Einstein's Discussion of Relativity and the Outer Cosmos?* and *The X-ray Defractometer applied to Modern Industrial Practice?* and for light bed-time reading I would like *Advanced Application of Digital Computers to Modern Office Practice.*" In due course I was able to supply her with the volumes asked for, and she thanked me and left. I

[1] p. 45.

thought at the time that the man she eventually married would have to be a D.Sc. or Ph.D. at least.'

From this story it is abundantly clear that his personality is quite up-side down. The masculine is living in a fantasy world, whilst his feminine side is altogether masculine. The feminine, which should be warm, instinctual and practical, is exaggeratedly intellectual; it has obviously taken possession of the personality of the man, he is hag-ridden, and therefore his masculine side was never able to develop and he remained in the infantile world of dreams. How could he possibly, under these circumstances, play the part of a man in life and cope with the woman? The fact that he remained in his infantile world of fantasy was borne out by his very considerable imagination, of which we have several examples in the material I quote.

He produced several psychological prescriptions, which unknown to him were in the tradition of the Alchemists.

Argentii Nitras gr. 4	Silver Nitrate 4 grains.
Aurii Chloride gr. 6	Gold Chloride 6 grains
Aq. Comm. ad. 12 drs.	Communal tap water up to 12 drms.
M ft. m. sec. art	Mix and make a mixture in the manner of the art of Pharmacy.
Mitte 6 fd. ozs.	Send 6 fluid ozs.
Sig. ½ fd. oz. t.i.d. Dur. dol.	Label ½ fluid oz. 3 times a day when pain is troublesome.

Silver is the metal and colour of the moon, the feminine. The number 4 is the square of 2, the feminine number.
Nitrum (from the Greek) is natural alkaline salt which is still used in the East as soap. We have seen already in the previous fantasy the need to cleanse the feminine which was so dominant in his life.
Gold is the metal and colour of the sun, the masculine. Three is the masculine number, and this he has doubled in his prescription.
Chloros (Greek) is the green of the grass, it is something alive, and it is the colour of the Holy Spirit, 'the Giver of Life'. The 'Rosarium' says,

'. . . because that greenness (viriditas) is straightway changed by our magistery into our most true gold.'

The prescription, working through the Holy Spirit, will effect in him the gold of true manhood, which is of course, the object of the thera-peutic exercise.
Common water is the cleansing water of Baptism, that is, the rebirth,

also it is 'common' in the sense of communal. This water is most necessary for the young man must find his place in the common life of the community, he must be well mixed. Further, he had over-compensated for his inferiority by giving himself, in his fantasies, most exalted positions such as President of the British Association and the Chairman of I.C.I. He must drink much of the *common* water.

The number 12 is very important for, as being 3 x 4, it signifies the combination of the masculine and the feminine in perfect unity. It is therefore the symbol of wholeness, perfection, and integration, and for which reason there were chosen Twelve Apostles, and the Heavenly City was given twelve gates, and twelve foundations, the twelve signs of the Zodiac and the twelve months of the year make the complete and perfect whole. Man is only whole when the masculine and the feminine sides of his personality are fused as one, when the Heavenly and the earthly meet as they did in the Incarnation.

The six fluid ounces, 2 x 3, is saying the same. The healing work is no magical and rapid cure, many small doses will have to be taken of the medicine of masculinity and of life.

A second prescription was:

Liq. Plumbii Subacet. Fort 2 dr.	Strong Lead Subacetate soln. 2 dr.
Pulve Rhei. Co. 10 gr.	Compound Rhubarb powder 10 gr.
Tinct. Zingib. Fort. ½ fd. oz.	Strong tincture of Ginger ½ oz.
Spt. Ammon. aromat 6 mms.	Aromatic spirit of Ammonia 6 mms.
Auric Chloride 1 dr.	Gold Chloride 1 dr.
Emulsifying ointment q.s.	Sufficient quantity.
Fiat Unguenta Sec. art.	Make an ointment according to the art of Pharmacy.
Sig. Ung. Prima Luce dur dol utende	To be used at first light when pain is troublesome.
Mitte 6 fd. ozs.	Send 6 fd. ozs.

Lead is the base metal from which the Alchemists sought to obtain gold; no base metal, no gold, which means that we have to accept our earthly instinctual side if we are to possess the gold, the most precious metal, of life. A 'Transforming Symbol' was required for this pur-pose—the Philosopher's Stone, and it is easy to see our Lord, Who came down to earth, as He Who transforms and uses our base metal. The down to earth side of our life is the feminine, hence the 2 drams in the prescription.

Rhubarb is the cleansing which is required, and this may be in place of the water as the symbol of Baptismal re-birth, and a considerable quantity of this is required.

The Ginger is a warming compound. The Alchemists are often seen in their old drawings with bellows heating up their furnaces in which the base metal has been placed. The patient himself has to supply some 'ginger' to the working out of his problem, although in the end it is found to be what we cannot but call 'the Spirit' Who has effected the transformation, for after all the transforming symbol is an experience which baffles description.

Ammonia, or Sal Volatile, is obviously a spiritual ingredient in the prescription, its reviving effect needs no comment.

Chloride of Gold has been mentioned in the previous prescription. This prescription is for an ointment, which brought to the mind of the prescriber the anointing nard of the Gospels. Anointing refers to the work of the Holy Spirit in healing. This is the psychotherapuetic nard, which nonetheless is a work of the Spirit.

'At first light' was interpreted by the prescriber as having a reference to the inner light of intuition which is brought to bear upon the mental pain.

These prescriptions spring from the Collective Unconscious, the reservoir of the great experiences in the history of man in which we all share at a deep unconscious level. His problem is such that it cannot be solved by simple conscious effort, or even by delving into the buried part of his personal history. We shall see something of this again in the later part of this chapter.

The young prescriber was anxious to say that the foregoing prescriptions are of psychological importance only, and that they are of no medical value whatever. If used as indicated they are poisonous.

I am including a dream in the selection of material from the analytic sessions because it shows clearly how something as mysterious as anything could be is coming to the aid of a very sick person, this time a woman. When the human predicament passes beyond a certain point conscious striving seems altogether futile, we are lost and the only hope lies in the appearance of a Saviour. This is often the borderland between sanity and insanity, consciousness and the abysmal depths of the archaic within the personality. The dream went as follows:

'Two men named David, one with a long beard, wanted me to go somewhere with them. I was worried and afraid about this since they would not say where it was, but they assured me that I would be quite alright, and so I went. We arrived in what must have been a foreign land, for it had hills and hardly any grass as the soil appeared to be sand. The two men stood with me looking as I went into the wilderness. Then a Rajah appeared, and the two men vanished. The Rajah said, "Will you please drive me to the land over the hills." When I looked I saw a car, and inside it was a box which turned out to be a coffin. I felt uneasy, but he said I had nothing to fear. The body inside the coffin was very precious. I went to the car, but could not start it, so the Rajah went a little way towards a steep hill and returned with an elephant. I asked him what he thought I was going to do with that, then he smiled and fetched the coffin which was so plain, it looked such a poor container for someone who must have been so precious. He told me to sit on the elephant's trunk, which I did, then he rested the coffin on my back, and then I realized that the Rajah was not going with me. I said, "I cannot go alone, for I don't know the way." He said, "You are not alone, and if you get into difficulty on your journey, I will be there." I started off on this journey. The coffin began to move from side to side, as if the body must still be alive. I was finding it hard work to keep going, and I thought many times I would give up, then the Rajah appeared from out of the blue, and he said, "Alright, I will help you now." I somehow felt I had failed the two men called David, but when I mentioned this he assured me that I had not, in fact, he said I had done well. So I got on the elephant's trunk behind the coffin. For a brief moment I thought the Rajah was the David with the beard, but then I thought he could not be; the elephant got up and we started on journey again.'

This presents a picture of the necessity both to help oneself and to rely on Someone greater than oneself, for without the Rajah there was no hope.

There were two Davids, as in the Bible account one part of David was human and sensuous, the other was the shepherd and spiritual guide of the people. These two Davids represented the dreamer's masculine images (her 'animus'), and the one with the beard represented the figure of our Lord.

The dreamer from her childhood had been possessed by the greatest fears, for her mother had used fear daily as the means by which she controlled her. This fear prevented her from going on the journey of life, thus she needed assurance at the very beginning, and she must learn to have faith, and live by faith, for the Davids could not tell her just where she was going.

The country to which she was being taken was foreign to her, it was barren and sandy like a wilderness. This was the journey into her own soul where there seemed, like the Gospel story, to be little grass in the place, that is, little of the creative work of the Spirit. The Rajah was briefly recognized at the end of the dream to be 'the man with the beard', and as the dream proceeds the Saviour figure becomes dominant. The 'land over the hills' is the new expanse of life that she is to discover. The Elephant, as a living thing, is substituted for the car, which is a dead thing and 'artificial', for there is no artificial and easy solution to her problem; she must grow to the solution of her life-journey. There is an affinity here with the 'night sea journey' which is set about with great danger, for it is the descent into the unconscious so that, through death, death may be conquered and life possessed. This is the coming face to face with the great Leviathan and a veritable entry into the dark and terrifying belly of the 'whale'. It is a journey which has to be made. The Elephant symbolizes the wisdom of the ages, for he never forgets, he is the wise creature and at the same time a representative of great instinctual (sexual) energy. The trunk, which she must hold on to, stands for a layer of her own psyche with which she is to be integrated.

The content of the coffin was most precious, and this clearly is the coffin containing her past dead self, and we note how that, as she proceeds, the deadness within becomes alive. This new aliveness causes her some apprehension, as is usual in the process of re-birth. The newly born looks back in longing to the mother, which is as dangerous as it is fascinating. The ancient Egyptian legend of Osiris tells of how, after the night sea journey, the coffin containing Osiris rested in the branches of a cedar-tree which encased it within its trunk. Isis eventually came to the rescue and restored Osiris by an act of reconstitution, as it were in a womb. The movement in the coffin in our dream sounds rather like the movements of the babe before its birth, and thus the theme is one of re-birth, the spiritual separation from the mother. Jung gives a reproduction of a Relief in which Osiris is seen in a cedar-coffin.[1]

The Rajah's assurance that she would not be alone brings to mind our Lord's words, 'Lo, I am with you always.'

There is clearly seen in this dream how that the really sick soul is completely powerless to help herself, everything depends upon factors outside the conscious human situation for her healing. Such indications inform the analyst of the prognosis of the case, and in the case of the 'borderline' patient an eye must always be kept on the symbolic material of the sessions. If the unconscious material produces such a figure of the Saviour archetype, it may equally well reveal that nothing but disaster will attend the continuance of the analysis, or that it should never be undertaken. The drawings of the patients will give similar information.

It may help to illustrate the latter position by quoting a piece of writing which was accompanied by a drawing, the work of another patient. Both the drawing and the writing reveal singular artistic

[1] Jung—*The Symbols of Transformation*, p. 237.

ability. You will note the complete absence of the Saviour archetype. This is what he wrote:

'I threw myself at the wall of the house, and out of the window I saw many black cats put their heads, and a huge black cat with yellow teeth cried, and the tears fell on the street below. And I cried and cried until I slid down the face of the wall and groped in the gutter, and I found a pool of water and put my head down and covered my face and tried to drown. But they pulled me out and put my head on a balcony, and I saw the crowds pass by. The mothers' weeping for their husbands, and their husbands for their children, and black waters streamed down the streets. So I cried still more, and threw my hair into the sky, and clutched at the roofs of the houses. The houses fell down and I wandered over the broken walls and broken floors and all that had fallen down, and the bones rattled, and the sky was dry, and I no longer cried. But the shutters banged, and the doors slammed, and the noise in that empty place was almost too loud to endure. O the poor cats. The poor people. The broken houses. I asked heaven for a fire to burn it all up, but nothing came. Perhaps a flood would wash it away, but the sky was clear, and the sun was miles away, and nothing possessed the place but the wind blowing out of the doors and in at the windows, and around and about until I was dizzy. Then I pulled at my head and split it in two, and I split my body, I split and split, with a foot on each side, and an eye on each side, one to think with, and one to wink with.'

This material, of course, was not analysed; it would have been too dangerous to do so. In a sense it is magnificent, magnificent as is the apocalyptic language of the Gospels:

'Immediately after the tribulation of those days shall the sun be darkened, and the moon shall not give her light, and the stars shall fall from heaven, and the powers of the heavens shall be shaken . . .'

(*St Matthew* XXIV, 29.)

In this case the Saviour appears on the clouds of heaven as the Son of Man.

A closer look at the writing reveals tragedy all through, and there is a repeated reaching out towards destruction. The house which should be a place of protection and comfort is disgorging evil and all that is sinister; against this house he throws himself in vain. The black cats are associated with witches, and the yellow teeth do not make the picture any prettier. Cats are symbols of the evil mother image (the 'anima'). The crying is everywhere and tragedy is the mood, in fact everything is so intolerable that he tries to drown himself, but he cannot die. His head is placed on a balcony, and the mourners go about the streets down which black waters stream. All is broken and fallen down, and it is no use clutching at the roofs; bones rattled, doors banged, the sky was dry—in fact it has passed crying over in the death of emotion, save that the noise of the emptiness was unendurable. The sun, the image of the good father, was miles away. Catastrophe alone remained, and a fearful state of splitting. Thoughts persist, but the other half has gone blind and dead, for it is 'winked at'.

Dissolution and catastrophe tell the tale of the deepest tragedy life can hold. Unless the therapist knows what he is about he can take people into such an abyss, by 'stepping in where angels fear to tread.' A good third of the people who come to me for help have to be turned away on account of it being dangerous to proceed analytically with them. The foremost requirement of the analyst is that he should be able to discern what disorders are safe to treat, what require utmost caution, and those which should be left alone and passed on to the psychiatrist.

These fantasies reveal a splitting of the personality to a considerable degree. Treatment may be given when it is a horizontal splitting, as in the case of the young man who produced the first material given in this chapter. His 'head' was seriously split off from his body and all that belongs to its instinctual life. In such a case the treatment will be expected to take a very long time, but given patience in patient and therapist alike a good measure of integration may take place.

In the last case given the splitting was vertical as was shown in a drawing he did. It was of a head with a wide V-shaped fissure from the top to the grossly distorted mouth. This is an instance of what should be left alone, except for the research worker in this field. As we have pointed out there is no Saviour, and the patient is without help in his soul, he feels completely undone. Drugs are the real friend for such people. But even here schizophrenia is found to be a strange disorder, for it can go as it came, in an unaccountable way. The psychotherapist, may I repeat, has to be aware of the signs which reveal a latent psychosis. This I consider to be a matter of utmost importance, for to continue the invasion of the unconscious in these conditions may well release material which the ego, in its weakness, cannot control, and the end is disaster.

Paintings as well as dream material, along with many overt symptoms, provide the warning signals, and in dealing with such people as possess these adverse signs it is far better to err on the side of caution. I have known of L.S.D. being used upon such a person with shattering consequences.

Returning to the material given above we see in the last instance an illustration of catastrophe which is final. We should always be watchful for dreams which end in tragedy, but in this case the tragedy is there all through, nothing else is known. Jung taught us to see the significance of this tragic material, he says:

'The primary symptom seems to have no analogy with any kind of functional disturbance. It is as if the very foundations of the psyche were giving way, as if an explosion or an earthquake were tearing the structure of a normally built house. I use this analogy on purpose, because it is suggested by the symptomatology of the initial stages. Sollier has given us a vivid description of these *troubles cénesthésiques*, which are compared to explosions, pistol-shots, and other violent noises in the head. They appear in projection as earthquakes, cosmic catastrophies, as the fall of the stars, the splitting of the sun, the falling asunder of the moon, the transformation of people into corpses, the freezing of the universe, and so on.'[1]

In a later paper on Schizophrenia he says:

'Whereas the neurotic can rely instinctively on his personality dissociation never losing its systematic character, so that the unity and inner cohesion of the whole are never seriously jeopardized, the latent schizophrenic must always reckon with the possibility that his very foundations will give way somewhere, that an irretrievable disintegration will set in, that his ideas and concepts will lose their cohesion and their connection with other spheres of association and with the environment. As a result, he feels threatened by an uncontrollable chaos of chance happenings. He stands on treacherous ground, and very often he knows it. The dangerousness of his situation often shows itself in terrifying dreams of cosmic catastrophes, of the end of the world and such things. Or the ground he stands on begins to heave, the walls bend and bulge, the solid earth turns to water, a storm carries him up into the air, all his relatives are dead, etc. These images bear witness to a fundamental disturbance of relationship, that is, of the patient's rapport with his surroundings, and geographically illustrate the isolation that menaces him.'[2]

[1] C. G. Jung—*The Psychogenesis of Mental Disease*, par. 522.
[2] Ibid, par. 599.

CHAPTER 8

EMOTION AND PHYSICAL HEALTH

Psychotherapeutic practice is an experience of mystery. The deeper the penetration of the psyche the more the therapist and patient alike realize that inexplicable workings and influences are being activated; although the less sick person will not have to undergo the dark journey into the depths. It is a fascinating experience when a patient brings forward the symbolic material, about which Jung has taught us so much, even though, as is often the case, the patient does not appreciate the power which lies behind it. It is then that the bounds of rational understanding are passed, and we move in a realm no longer dominated by the phases of cause and effect. The world of the psychotherapist is altogether different from that of the neurologist, who can only interpret experience in the light of physical changes, and who, like the Pavlovian, sees the mechanics of the mind, and consequent upon this the experience of thought and feeling. He seems not to realize that this way of seeing things, on his theory, must be nothing but the product of the individual *physical* transformations in his own thought processes, and that it makes nonsense of all thought and experience.

Nowhere is the effect of feeling upon the mechanics and chemistry of the body so clearly seen as in psychosomatic disorders, where the emotional life of the person is obviously prior to the physical expression of the dis-ease. In these cases the physical aspect entirely disappears when the patient attends to his emotional problems, and often the physical equivalents may be produced in the analytic session. I have witnessed rashes come and go, the onset of violent toothache which has come on with all the suddenness of the pressing of an electric switch, and the production of pains in the head, back, stomach, eyes, ears and legs. Asthma attacks, paralysis of limbs, lumps in the throat, body odours, coldness and perspiration, vomiting and nausea —all following the patterns of emotional causation.

A most interesting case was that of a woman who was convinced that she was having a baby, in spite of being told to the contrary after numerous examinations by her doctor and the hospital. Nothing would shake her in this opinion, for she said she could feel perfectly well the movements of the baby, lactation was taking place, and, of course, her periods for the past months had ceased. What so much puzzled her was the fact that through a physical illness she had not been near her husband, and therefore the child must be by the Holy Ghost. I offered to investigate her emotional condition, but she insisted there was nothing to investigate, and that the only unusual thing about her was that she was having a baby by the Holy Ghost.

Freud catalogued the anxiety equivalents as: disorders of the heart, which included palpitation with short arhythmia (irregularity), long lasting tachycardia (rapid heart beat) and pseudo angina pectoris; disorders of breathing, such as asthma and several forms of dyspnoea (breathlessness): excessive sweating, trembling and shaking, bulimia (morbid hunger), often with giddiness: locomotor giddiness, and muscular cramps, and bladder and bowel irregularities.

Stekel added to this list: the breathlessness of air-hunger; oncoming weariness amounting to faintness; deadness of fingers, hand and arm; migraine, and great restlessness; numerous digestive and throat disturbances, with periodic emaciation and convulsions; muscular tics, pains and cramps; psychological vertigo and pseudo-epilepsy, sleeplessness, fainting, and stuttering.

A good picture of what the emotions can do with the body is given in Stekel's description of an 'anxiety attack'[1]:

'The patients feel that their end is approaching, they fear a stroke, feel that something is entangled in their brain, their heads feel as if they would burst; they are going mad, their hearts seem to stop, somebody is throttling them and interferes with their breathing; just as a dying man must feel. All the symptoms that usually accompany the effect of fear or horror may also accompany an attack. The patients pale, lose their balance, and must lie down. They fight in vain for words and breath. Arms and legs shake as in fever. Many patients shake violently, sweat breaks out from the whole body, the hair bristles, and the back creeps with coldness. . . . The pupils of the eyes dilate. The secretion of saliva ceases to flow, and the mouth becomes dry. Often there follow attacks of faintness, migraine, giddiness or tachycardia of great intensity, various pains occur in the heart, chest, head; neuralgia, stomach ache and so on. All these phenomena can appear in the simplest to the gravest form, isolated, or in manifold combinations and variations.'

How often I hear people say to such a description of the physical effects of the emotional life. 'That is a perfect picture of my illness, or of what I had years ago, but I was never told that it could have been psychological in origin, why was this?' I shall not attempt to answer this question, except to say that new ideas are usually met

[1] *Conditions of Nervous Anxiety*, p. 15.

with prejudice, and that this is likely to be found as much in the medical profession as in my own. Prejudice, especially when it is based upon fear, dies very hard. I can do no better than quote Dr Franz Alexander of America, who is one of the people most responsible for bringing this aspect of medicine into the open in the last thirty years. He writes:

'Some sound and conservative clinicians deem this a threat to the foundations of medicine so arduously acquired, and authoritative voices warn the profession that this new "psychologism" is incompatible with medicine as a natural science. They would prefer that medical psychology remain restricted to the field of medical art, to tact and intuition in handling the patient, as distinct from the scientific procedure of therapy proper based on physics, chemistry, anatomy, and physiology.'[1]

If this is true of American medicine how much more so of this country where psychology is not taken very seriously, save perhaps by a younger generation of medical men.

Further, Dr Alexander would be the last person to dispute the therapeutic results of the 'spiritual' approach to certain types of illness. Again he writes:

'Once the healing functions, mental and physical, were united in one hand. Whatever the explanation of the healing power of the medicine man or the evangelist or of the Holy Water of Lourdes, there is little doubt that these agents achieved a spectacular curative effect upon the sick, in certain respects even more dramatic than many of our drugs which we can analyse chemically and the pharmacological effects of which we know with great precision.'[2]

A psychosomatic disorder is a radical combination of emotional and physical factors. It may be true to say that in every disease emotional factors play a part, and that illness is multicausal. The doctor's success with his patient must be attributable in part to the rapport between him and his patient, and when this rapport breaks down the sooner the patient changes his doctor the better it will be for all concerned. However, the common view persists that the body is a machine which at times needs a mechanic, in the form of the doctor, to put it right. A frequent criticism of psychotherapy is that it is mysticism, and by this is meant that it is all 'airy-fairy', in contrast with the solid facts of neurology and biochemistry. Thus the illness is viewed as something separate from the sufferer. It is surprising how little is known about the causation of much illness,

[1] *Psychosomatic Medicine*, Ch. 1.
[2] Ibid., Ch. 1.

which leaves open the possibility of non-physical factors as being at least contributory to the origin of the disorder.

There is more emotion operative in life than we care to recognize, and the full significance of this may only be seen when we realize that emotional experiences are accompanied by physiological changes. For example, fear sets the heart palpitating, it decreases the quantity of hydrochloric acid in the stomach and stimulates the flow of bile: anger increases the activity of the heart, raises the blood pressure and effects changes in carbohydrate metabolism. Amongst the more obvious physical changes are the blush of shame or the flush of anger, the tears of sorrow, and the muscular agitation in 'excitement' or anxiety.

It has also been pointed out that sufferers from specific disorders reveal a definite character pattern, thus the migraine patient is often an exacting person, peptic ulcers are associated with people who worry, colitis bespeaks an over-tidy and clean type of person, asthmatics reveal themselves to be persons who suffer from an over-protective and domineering kind of mother.

This body-mind relationship was first detected by Freud during his researches into hysteria. Conversion Hysteria is a disorder which is unconsciously produced to express repressed emotions. It is a feature of these dramatic illnesses that they operate along ideational paths, that is, they are functions which have an end in view, and thus their area is that of the will and sense perception. Certain physiological processes are set in motion when a specific purpose is designed, as, for example, when we wish to strike someone and the arm is raised. But when the desire is repressed, along with its attendant emotion, there is no discharge in action; nevertheless the emotions are unconsciously activating the physical processes. The desire may now only be expressed symbolically in the physical field by, for example, rheumatoid arthritis or paralysis of the arm. The person remains in a chronic state of tension without any discharge of energy. These disorders are the symbolic expression of aggressive and self-assertive desires which have been repressed or inhibited. The symptoms use some of the repressed or inhibited energy, and they also act as a kind of defence against an action which would produce guilt. Rheumatoid arthritis would then be a defence against hostile action towards someone, and further the suffering could fulfil the need for self-punishment as an act of atonement for the guilt laden desire.

An altogether different group of disorders known as 'stress' have their origin in the vegetative organs (concerned with growth and nutrition), and they operate through the automatic nervous system (independently functioning). These disorders are not ideational, products of the will, as are Conversion ailments; they have no association with design or aim. Their origin is found in the way in which emotional influences stimulate or inhibit any organ of the vegetative function, for example, fear affects the adrenal gland from which follow a chain of reactions. Should the emotion become repressed the glandular stimulation becomes permanent, and from this a chronic disorder follows known as an 'organ neurosis' or a functional disorder. These disorders, then, do not express or symbolize the original emotion, but are due to the constant stimulation of an organ by a permanent emotional state, to give another example, as when repressed rage sets up acidosis.

The effect of living in the atomic age, in high geared society, or the effect of experiencing a breakdown of family life, or life just having lost its meaning, can produce stress where the situation gives rise to fear, hostility, guilt or frustration, and the emotion is repressed or inhibited. Other situations may likewise produce a sense of inferiority, jealousy, envy, anger or worry. An inner conflict may also arise between a repressed natural urge and a condemning conscience (Super Ego). The particular form the stress takes acts as a kind of psychological indicator, in that the part of the body which is affected gives a clue as to what is happening. An affected heart will lead us to explore the possibility that repressed rage is the cause; disturbances of the respiratory function may lead us to investigate the person's emotional living space; constipation may be but one symptom of a constipated personality, and it may be found that the person is holding himself in, and is a self-protective type. In simple cases, where the stress has been set up by a bad relationship with the immediate environment, it may be removed by a change of circumstances.

The emotional disorders of the autonomic nervous system are divided into two types according to whether the sympathetic or parasympathetic nervous system is involved. The sympathetic reactions relate to our dealings with the outside world, whilst the parasympathetic deal with our internal affairs. A situation arises in the external world to which we respond by fight or flight, and to this end the automatic processes of the body operate, activating some functions and inhibiting others to expedite the exercise. On the other hand the response may be one of withdrawal and the functions of inner maintenance and upbuilding take over, which is the function of the parasympathetic system. These are passing phases in ordinary life, but in the sick person these processes have become chronic on account of repressed emotions. Where there is a sympathetic reaction the disorders will be related to activity, and they will be such as migraine, hypertension, hyperthyroidism, cardiac neuroses, fainting, arthritis, and possibly diabetes. In the case of a parasympathetic reaction the disorder may be a peptic ulcer, constipation, diarrhoea, colitis, asthma, fatigue states. Thus stress symptoms tell us much about what is happening in the unconscious. It is obvious that where there is psychological causation the treatment should be psychotherapy. However, there should be expected a kind of complicity between the psychic and somatic elements, and the body is expected to show a predisposition to certain paths of reaction. For example, a certain psychic condition produces an asthmatic attack in one person whereas the same condition in another does not. The body's contribution may be a specific allergen; but here again, who can say what constitutes allergy? I have treated many cases of asthma and in every case, with finished treatment, they have become free from their complaint through psychotherapy.

It will be well to illustrate in detail what has been said, and since disorders of the appetite and eating are so common these have been chosen. But first, something must be said by way of background, in view of the great importance of feeding to the infant. His earliest life is almost wholly concerned with food, his first discomfort is doubt-less hunger, and a warm glow of security and well-being is felt when that hunger is met. He feels that he is being sustained in his strange and frightening world by being held close to a warm and responding source of life. Food becomes equated with love, and if he is fortunate every feeding is a love-feast, and thereby fear is dispelled. Thus food has a value far beyond its capacity to satisfy hunger, and any threat to its supply will be viewed with utmost apprehension, if not with sheer panic. A threat to the supply of food will be met by an increased demand for it, and when this demand is unconscious it will show it-self by greed which may well extend towards everything in later life. He will then be envious of all who seem to have what he has not, jealous of rivals, real or imagined, possessive, demanding, ambitious, and thrifty to the extent of meanness, and in his acquisitiveness he may well be aggressive or hostile. He revealed his aggression as a baby in his biting. Melanie Klein has shown, as Stekel did before her, the extent to which envy and hostility can go in the infant's fantasy life. In order to possess or control his external objects the infant puts them into his mouth and thus incorporates them into himself, which means that in his fantasies he has filled his stomach with objects which now have become dangerous and hostile to him, and very considerable guilt is experienced.

The infant's greatest experience of pleasure comes through sucking, with the result that food becomes associated with this kind of pleasure, but when there is a breakdown in feeding it is naturally felt to be a privation of pleasure, with strong emotional reactions following. Pleasure is part of the birthright of man and serious trouble follows when he feels robbed of this.

The various intense emotions which feeding can arouse are likely to be repressed, which in certain cases stimulate the bodily nutritive processes for action without the action taking place. Thus the bodily processes are thrown out of balance, and there follows a permanent state of tension. For example, infantile rages prepare the body for an expenditure of an immense amount of energy, which remains un-expended on account of their repression; and this would-be out-going activity inhibits the digestive processes. Guilt, which is associated with aggressive incorporative fantasies, often prevents the reception of the food for which the body is prepared; likewise disgust has an inhibitory effect. Some years later in life we may find the young person suffering from nutritional disturbances which have been caused by sexual inhibitions, and the explanation for this seems to lie in a regression from the later sexual pleasure, which has become inhibited, to the earlier pleasure obtained in the sucking phase.

Loss of appetite, periodic or chronic, is a frequent occurrence both in neuroses and psychoses, and may at times be given the name of anorexia nervosa. The many individual variants make it difficult to deal with digestive disturbances in general, but when a person has patently an oral problem it is reasonable to assume the disorder to be an emotional one. Loss of appetite may go back to the beginning of life when the baby was 'a difficult feeder', which may have been due to the infant's difficulty in adapting himself to a separate existence. The fact that many patients put on weight during an analysis supports the contention that the emotional condition affects the digestive processes, or the appetite. One patient who came to me in an emaciated state has since put on three stones in weight. Another person is recovering her appetite as we explore her early incorporative fantasies along Kleinian lines. The act of eating unconsciously repre-sents and repeats the savage criminal acts directed towards the source of food, and which are often the expression of envy and jealousy. In view of this it is understandable that guilt of the blackest hue attends the daily acts of feeding, and that this may be so intense that a bad conscience prevents the acceptance of food altogether. Fasting has long been a sign of repentance.

In other cases of feeding difficulties the baby may prepare the ground for the later hard-luck view of life, which besides inducing self-pity also stimulates anger. It is sometimes found that when a child refuses food he is doing it in order to be able to pity himself, and perhaps make the refusal of food a stick with which to beat his parents. Parents are always concerned if the child goes off his food, and therefore loss of appetite may be a means of drawing considerable attention to oneself. These various considerations go to show that each case must be treated individually.

There is a variant of the above in which the young person is unable to eat in the presence of certain people. This is a condition usually found in girls, and they go off their food in the presence of the father or other men. Sexual fantasies account for this.

Since the refusal of food may be an act of atonement for deep guilt, it would be dangerous to force a person to eat, for then they might take to a more dangerous, and indeed final, form of self-punishment. But even if such action does not lead to this, it will only lead him to commit further fantasy crimes which will greatly aggravate his condition and increase the guilt.

Bulimia is the disorder which is symptomatic of the opposite emotional condition, where the appetite is grossly exaggerated. In the great majority of such cases the origin is a psychological one, and it is derived from an excessive unconscious demand for food through the person in infancy being deprived of food or love. The insatiable appetite may also be based upon an angry devouring of the breast, or again, upon the feeling that nothing ever came his way, so he fills himself full on every possible occasion. In other cases there may be unconscious pregnancy fantasies in which food has become synonymous with babies.

Another condition is that of nervous vomiting, in which the food is rejected after it has been eaten, and not before, as is the case in anorexia. Guilt may demand that what has been eaten or stolen is surrendered, or disgust at what has been incorporated in fantasy may cause the vomiting. Hypochondriacs are afraid of what they have eaten or might eat. An unconscious rejection of fantasied or actual pregnancy may be the cause of the vomiting. In all such cases the analysing-out of the emotional life is the only satisfactory treatment.

We must also mention esophageal neuroses, in which people find it difficult to swallow, the food just will not go down. In other people there is the psychological lump (globus hystericus) which prevents the act of swallowing. It may represent a symbolic refusal to assimilate essential information, when, with acceptance, the lump vanishes. On the other hand the person may be standing mid-way between not eating and rejecting what he has eaten—an attempt to make the best of both worlds. In this case there are likely to be very primitive sexual fantasies, in which there is a mixture of wanting and disgust at wanting.

Finally there are gastric neuroses, and here we are immediately confronted with a variety of possible causes; for example, the bill may be sent in for prolonged bad eating habits, which, in their turn, may have a psychological origin in psychic restlessness or impatience. The greedy people whom we have been discussing will obviously overtax the digestion, or the trouble may be due to acidosis caused by unconscious hostility, or a host of other causes. It has been found that in these gastric neuroses an early dependent, hungry, help-seeking attitude to life is involved; but such dependence is felt to be inconsistent with the need to be an adult, with a healthy independence. It is easy to be angry with oneself in these circumstances.

An illustration of the conflict may be found in the story of the Exodus. The Hebrews passed through the Red Sea on dry land (*Exodus* XIV), but this was no true Baptism, for their attachment to the past remained. This may account for the subsequent story, for soon they were looking back to Egypt with longing. The new life, with all its demands and responsibilities, seemed to be a worse state than the first. At least in Egypt they were cared for, and it was in the interests of the taskmasters to keep them alive; but this wilderness was sheer struggle for survival, and who knew what new perils the next day would bring? The new life at first appeared as hard and barren as the wilderness. They had to learn very painfully that God was with them, and that He would provide manna and water for the journey to the Promised Land. One wonders how many peptic ulcers those Hebrews suffered during those forty years of wandering in the wilderness! We have full evidence of their anger towards Moses, whom we can symbolize, in the wider canvas of life, as the part of themselves rightly set on independence and freedom. Moses would also represent the driving ambition which is characteristic of many ulcer cases.

This ancient story is still being re-enacted during the analysis of the patient, for his resentment at being brought out of his own private Egypt, his status quo, is often projected on to his analyst, his Moses. Our Lord's reference to putting the hand to the plough and not looking back (*St Luke* IX, 62) could well refer to everyman's private Egypt. He Himself bore the bad projections of those He came to deliver from their bondage.

We have, then, in this ancient story of the Exodus a typical picture of what is calculated to produce a gastric disorder, and a peptic ulcer in particular. There is the desire to be dependent and cared for, and the conflicting pride which puts on self-sufficiency and ambition. Such people are usually aggressive, and they are inclined to overburden themselves. Harry in Chapter 2 is the type of person we have in mind. Unconsciously they seek support, but consciously they spurn help; unconsciously they want to snuggle close and warm to the all-providing mother, consciously they must be here, there, and everywhere in the world of affairs.

However, some people will not play the self-sufficient part, and overtly they are the clinging type. Where things have gone wrong with such people is that life has not supported them in the way they desire; there are no props or people upon whom they can lean. The deep frustration of their need for support stimulates chronically the stomach functions. Both spoiling and genuine privation in infancy can produce the demand for nutritive support. The anger arises when the great demand is not met. It is obvious that in these conditions there will be considerable gastric activity, and equal unbalance, for the stomach is ever being prepared to receive food which never comes. As we have already said, in the last analysis, the food is a symbol of love; this means that such disorders may symbolize an expectancy for love which never comes, and we can well understand how frustrated love turns to hate.

The consideration which we have given to gastric disorders is but one of many such accounts of psychosomatic illness we could have given. The emotional element in the disorder is plain to see, however much there may have been a physical predisposition in favour of the particular form of illness. It should be added, however, after a time physical damage may be caused which will call for medical and surgical aid. But given such treatment, the basic cause will not have been removed.

It is hoped that this discussion will have demonstrated the relevance of the Ministry to the mind and 'soul' of man to the cure of much 'physical' disorder. It has been established beyond all doubt that bad emotions and inner conflicts set up disease. How can anyone say that these root emotions are outside the range of the Christian Ministry? It is being suggested that since the emotions are being recognized as causative of certain illnesses, these emotions are the prerogative of the medical profession, but if the Church agrees that she must not interfere in this realm then she is allowing her sphere of influence to be grossly narrowed. These illnesses are directly related to guilt and anger, 'envy, hatred, malice and all uncharitableness,' pride, self-love and pretence; are we therefore to keep aloof from these destructive emotions because they have medical implications? Never for a moment would we cross over the border into the realm of pure medicine, and in so far as the body's disorder is a physical matter, the doctor, humanly speaking, must have the last word. But wherever emotional factors are fundamentally involved the Church has every right to enter the therapeutic situation. She must reveal the deep emotional sores of infection which are slowly, but surely, poisoning the whole life of the person, and, through him, the community. The conscious mind will play its important part, and the person will doubtless need all the courage he can muster, and all the Grace he can receive to reorientate his life and accept the forgiving love of God so freely offered. But when all this is done in many cases there remains a deeper problem to be faced, and unless this deep hidden sore is healed there can be neither peace nor wholeness.

The responsibility of the Church for the pernicious emotions of her members no more ceases when these emotions are banished from consciousness to the underworld of the unconscious, than does that of the criminal when he manages to ignore his crime. It is no answer to cover up the Stygian morass and pretend it is not there, and our Lord's strong words about whited sepulchres (*St Matthew* XXIII, 27) should be heeded. Merely to push unacceptable thoughts and feelings into the limbo of our private underworld only makes them the more insidious, for then their undermining and corrupting influences are beyond the control of consciousness.

Thus the Church must fulfil her responsibility in this matter, for she has the means at her disposal to perform a unique service in the healing of a man. To neglect to do so by reason of fear or prejudice is something for which someday she would have to give an account to her Lord.

CHAPTER 9

CO-OPERATION

The word co-operation is a fine one, and one which by its derivation suggests work and action, but it is a word which can be over-worked, and, becoming a cliché, leads to no resultant action whatever. It is as though we all give three cheers for co-operation, and then proceed to carry on in the same way as before. It is no use at all discussing co-operation if people are set in their habits and unbending in their prejudices, which they may prefer to call 'convictions'. Still less use is it if one side or the other feels that it has a monopoly. The 'closed shop' is a kind of mania to which the medical profession is as much prone as the Church. Fortunately in many quarters the Church is alive to the damage this has done, and still does.

In many parts of the country there have been efforts to draw together the doctors and the clergy, and from a point of view of fellowship and mutual understanding I am sure there has been a great gain in this. But this is not really what we mean by co-operation.

Very many doctors quietly ask the local parson or minister, with whom they are on the best of terms, to have a word with Mrs Bloggs or George Brown, and he goes along and really helps in the healing situation. This is co-operation so far as it goes, but it does not go nearly far enough.

In the previous chapter we showed from the findings of recent research that sickness cannot be separated from the person who is sick, and that in very many cases the symptoms of the disorder arise from the sick emotions of the person rather than from a mechanical breakdown within his constitution. Before co-operation between doctors and clergy can be set on a solid foundation both doctors and clergy would have to agree upon this, and it would call for considerable hard thinking and much courage on both sides. If I am not mistaken the medical profession is becoming increasingly aware of the emotional factors in sickness, which is necessarily making them see sickness on a wider front.

The work of the St Margaret's Clinic for Pastoral Psychology was undertaken eleven years ago by a group of clergy specially trained for the practice of psychotherapy, and all the treatment was given by them alone. When borderline cases turned up, or when people were psychotic, a consultant psychiatrist saw the patient, but apart from this we worked alone. It would have been a fine thing if, freed from the constant pressing duties of parish priests, we had been able to keep the patients' doctors well informed. This is advisable whenever possible for it both gives the doctor confidence in the treatment, and removes his misunderstandings in the case of a patient who cannot or will not co-operate. It is so easy for anyone to regard psychotherapy as a treatment in the ordinary sense of the word, whereas in fact the patient must always treat himself, with the aid of the therapist. In recent times I have been able to keep in better touch with the patients' doctors, although I have been surprised to find how many of my patients have no doctor, or simply do not consult him regarding their symptoms.

In my former book I suggested that the Church should have two specialist psychotherapists in each diocese. Commenting upon this a doctor said what we need is two in each deanery. This was obviously having in mind his own surgery, where neurotics gather who give no peace and waste much valuable time. I am sure that if the Church could only convince the medical profession of her competence to deal effectively with such people it would be only too pleased for us to take them. Besides the waste of precious time, these people cost the country a vast sum of money in tranquillizers which, when all is said and done, are no cure whatever. But if the Church can, by means of this ministry, make a new man out of a mere shadow of a self then it will be to the Glory of God, and to the immense benefit of every facet of society.

There is little doubt that as the therapeutic ministry becomes recognized as a radical healing function of the Church, as her Lord intended, then even two specialist therapists in a deanery will be far from adequate. In a real sense healing is the work of every man ordained to the ministry of the Church, and therefore the parish should be the healing centre. Given the vision of this great healing service it might well be that many young men, who now never give a thought to the possibility of ordination, will see this work to be their true vocation, and in this case the problem of the staffing of the large parishes might well be met.

The fact that some doctors from time to time send me their patients goes to show that they themselves are at a loss to know what to do with these emotionally sick people, and at the same time they realize that the troubles should be treated by other techniques. I hope I have made it abundantly clear in my earlier book that by a more 'spiritual' approach to these disorders people can be helped into a newness of life, and that this kind of treatment is something essentially different from that which is obtainable under the National Health Service.

Training

I am approached by clergy from all parts of the world wanting to know how they can be trained for this ministry. I have had to write many discouraging letters, for the simple reason that the Church has not yet become aware of the importance of the work, and the need to organize the training of therapists. Dr Frank Lake of Nottingham has done, and is still doing, a great piece of work in acquainting many clergy with this field, but at the best he helps the clergy to become 'Counsellors' and not psychotherapists. The latter function requires a training which takes several years. Yet without this more specialist ministry the Counselling will be weakened and it will be in a state where 'a little knowledge is a dangerous thing.' Since the younger generation of clergy are fast becoming psychologically minded the matter of training specialists is of special urgency. No co-operation with the doctors worthy of the name is likely in this sphere until the clergy are *adequately* equipped to offer the service. I shudder to think of vast numbers of clergy opening wide their arms to all sorts and conditions of emotionally sick people. Such a policy asks for the gravest trouble to descend upon the Church, the parson, and the 'patient', and can only in the end bring the whole ministry into disrepute and so sabotage all our efforts towards an effective co-operation with the doctors.

It is helpful to send a suitable and interested cleric along to a mental hospital for a period, for the insight and knowledge gained will be considerable. It will help him to recognize psychotic conditions, but this simply will *not* equip him as a psychotherapist. What he will learn in the hospital will not turn him into an analyst, for the kind of therapy we envisage for the Church is not practised in such places. Psychiatry, which is wholly a medical preserve, and psychotherapy are two different fields of treatment, and it is quite wrong to imagine that a priest, by rubbing shoulders with a psychiatrist, even if he is allowed to be so close, will automatically be turned into a kind of medical minor prophet. The whole training must be organized by the Church, either by setting up its own training centre, or by making it possible for selected men to receive full training elsewhere. However, it is easy to say 'elsewhere', for the only place I know where training is given is at 'The Open Way', Queen Anne Street, where the training is 'non-party'. Universities do not give degrees in psychotherapy.

It might not be out of place to mention what is involved in this specialist training by referring to the training I received. After a considerable reading of the subject I was permitted to attend diagnostic sessions for a year, during which time my reading of the subject was intensified. After this I undertook to treat certain cases myself under the strictest supervision. All the material of each session was very carefully worked over by my teacher, so that a session of one hour with the patient, on account of the later supervision, often extended to many hours. This went on for some three years, by which time I began to feel sufficiently able to treat my cases alone. Proper training must always be of this order. It should be added that if the training is to be found 'outside' the Church the expense of training each person will be between £2,000 and £3,000.

Another question which I am asked is regarding the suitability of people for their training. Many people are attracted to psychotherapy for the wrong reason, in that they are hoping unconsciously to solve their own problems in its pursuit. This makes one question the right of anyone to set himself up as a practising therapist, even if he has acquired a fair amount of psychological knowledge and some of the 'know how'. The Church has standards, and enquiries are made into the suitability of a person before his training for the ministry, and a similar test of suitability needs to be established by the Church in regard to this aspect of her ministry.

Therapy and the Church

When one has seen the effectiveness of this ministry in meeting the needs of sick people[1] a new vision of the Church is created, although, in fact, it is but the recovery of a vision that has long been lost. The Church is set amongst people who today come under the description given by the Prophet concerning those of his day—'the whole head is sick, the whole heart faint.' The need for this help is staggering in its magnitude, and the tragedy is that no actual cure is being offered to people, alleviation, yes; but not a cure.

Even the weakest imagination will see how the life of the Church could be transformed and strengthened. After my course of lectures at Leicester Cathedral I was asked whether it would be possible to hold a course of talks for parents in which help would be given with the many problems which children present. This is a field of supreme importance, and it would be of untold benefit to the Church if she could meet the great need. Why should not the Mothers' Union and the Young Wives' Fellowship be doing this kind of work which no one else is doing on a large scale? Surely it is just the kind of thing that should thrill the imagination on account of its arresting and vital relevance and urgency ! Then the organizations would be alive with purpose, and the perpetual headache about finding speakers and

---

[1] Cf. my *Christian Therapy*, inter al.

keeping them together by means of outings and parties would vanish overnight. Prospective mothers could be helped with the latest methods of childbirth, and in these and many other ways the Church would become re-vitalized, and seen to be most relevant to the human situation.[1]

The Church unquestionably was founded to be a healing Church, and yet she is preoccupied with a thousand and one things, doubtless important in their way, whilst this aspect of her essential Ministry is soft-pedalled or ignored. Like Martha, she is 'cumbered about with much serving,' particularly on committees, to such a degree that it appears obsessional; whilst the vision of the Church as a huge psycho-therapeutic centre for the ills of men, the Healing Body of Christ, seems to be entirely missing. After all her charge is the 'cure of souls', which is the care of sick souls, and the fact is that this is being done in the feeblest of ways, and that almost by accident. If we take our stand upon the Gospels and the Ministry of the Primitive Church we must confess our neglect of a great part of the Commission that Christ gave us. It should be as natural to come to the Church for the healing of depression and phobias, stress and obsessions, anxieties and perversions as to come to her to have babies baptized. Before this can happen, and sooner or later it must come to this, the Church may have to say to herself, 'Physician heal thyself.'

[1] See Appendix.

CHAPTER 10

THEOLOGY AND PSYCHOLOGY

Psychology is an empirical science, and within its domain any doctrine or theory irrelevant to the human situation is deemed to have no significance. It is because of this that psychological insights are of considerable importance to religion and its theology. Theology can be theoretical, metaphysical, without any reference to experience, or it can be of utmost value to the sick and whole alike. The therapist is often amazed at the way in which a patient versed in the Scriptures will show the relevance of the remotest corner of the Bible, even the Books of Chronicles and Kings come alive. The reason for this is that the Bible came into being out of human experience, and therefore it is always ready to speak to man. The way in which this is done is often beyond the scope of rational understanding, where the power and value reside in archetype and myth. Rationalism but destroys the symbols, and man thereby loses a life-line.

It is felt that something might be said with profit about the recent trends in the theological world entirely from the psychotherapist's empirical point of view. He has the right to be heard for he has his own kind of authority, which is neither theorizing nor an imposition of certain patterns upon life. It carries weight because it is of the nature of scientific discovery and at the same time a revelation of the depths of the personal.

The Bishop of Woolwich's book *Honest to God* has much which must be applauded. It is a monumental expression of freedom, about which we have been concerned in the previous chapters. Authority is under fire in the shape of Tradition, which, we have shown, is often used as an imposition, therefore it is fair set to wound the mind. It is an honest book, and honesty is a close relation of truth. Psychotherapy is predominately concerned with truth, and honesty is the basis of its work. Pretence and unreality destroy wholeness and make recovery impossible. The courage displayed in the book is its own commendation, and courage is essential if man is prepared to come to terms with life. Further, this book bids us look within, and unless religion is found on the inward side of life, in the depths of experience, it is worth very little. Love is, as *Honest to God* repeatedly stresses, the only adequate foundation in life and for purposeful living, love being the most personal part of life, and where God is known most intimately and fully. And how right it is to try to commend the Christian Way to unbelievers in language they understand. The various essays by The Reverend H. A. Williams express the same attitude.

Having paid a well-merited tribute there is, on the other side, criticism to be made. Such criticism as is made here is not given on theoretical theological grounds but what arises out of the findings of many years of intensive psychotherapeutic practice not only in my own case, but also in the much longer experience of The Reverend E. W. P. Ingham, until recently Chaplain of St Andrew's Hospital, Northampton. We could not allow the present trends to pass without comment.

The basic division within religious experience is that which William James made long ago when he divided people into the Once-born and the Twice-born. The Bishop tells us that he is one of the Once-born, and this is clearly so for it explains his religious standpoint.

The Once-born are understood when we see them in their first experience of life at the breast. A close, loving, satisfying, supporting feeling filled the baby with a glow of well-being, and he grew up feeling secure come what may, and he adventured forth into life. He may become a space-man or a great adventurer in the realm of ideas, he can run all the risks of isolation and all the threats of authority. He can happily burn his boats, because within him is unfailing strength, and inexhaustible supplies. He has much to give and to share with others without any risk of being emptied.

It is otherwise with the Twice-born, for from their earliest days they had no feelings of belonging, therefore they were insecure and afraid, their objects were remote or inaccessible, and life was cold. These people will be found for ever seeking support, and they will hang on to everything which is abiding and unchanging. Naturally authority is a safe stronghold which, when questioned, throws them into a state of anxiety. Tradition must not be questioned, the Bible and the Church must stand as firm as a rock.

For the Once-born prayer will seem less vital than for the Twice-born, Holy Communion may seem to be much less of a necessity. But for those whose earliest hunger went unsatisfied the offer of the Bread which cometh down from heaven, and the cup which will satisfy eternally makes an immediate appeal. The earliest experiences colour all subsequent experience. This will help us to understand the reactions of people to *Honest to God*. Those to whom it appeals are likely to be the deeply satisfied people, who look within themselves in depth and find peace and satisfaction there, whereas those who are hurt by it are likely to be the people who dare not look within themselves, and whose needs must hold fast to an unchanging environment and modes of thought. In the one case a person will be comforted by the book, and in another they will be tormented.

Our Cambridge friends find support in Freud's condemnation of religion on the grounds that it is a matter of projection. The 'out there' is a mirror image of what is really within, and therefore, it is argued, that the 'out there' is a mirage with which we can dispense and become more realistic in the process. Without going into a discussion of Freud's personal problems, we would point out that we live by our projections and that we cannot separate them from life. Identification with a good image or object is part of the process of growth, and even when the object carries the projection of an inner good image it still serves a constructive purpose. Projection of our good images upon God is inevitable, and doubtless our knowledge of God grows in this way. We can know nothing but what is part of our own experience.

Jung has much to say about the importance of symbols, and much therapeutic work can only be done by means of them. These symbols are essentially irrational. A criticism we have to make of the thought under discussion is that a deliberate attempt is made to limit the religious appeal to a single function of the personality, and to ignore the other three. Why should we so limit ourselves and comply with the dangerous trend in twentieth-century experience? Demythologizing is bringing disaster upon us, and we should not help on the process by destroying or discarding the symbols. Man needs them more than ever before.

Jung wrote in his *Memories, Dreams, Reflections*[1]: 'Myth is the natural and indispensable intermediate stage between unconscious and conscious cognition.'[2]
'Critical rationalism has apparently eliminated, along with so many other mythic conceptions, the idea of life after death. This could only have happened because nowadays people identify themselves almost exclusively with their consciousness, and imagine that they are only what they know about themselves. Yet anyone with only a smattering of psychology can see how limited this knowledge is. Rationalism and doctrinairism are diseases of our time: they pretend to have all the answers. But a great deal will yet be discovered which our present limited view would have ruled out as impossible.'[3]
'No science will ever replace myth, and a myth can be made out of any

---

[1] Jung's last work appeared after this book was written and these and the following quotations were added at the proof stage.
[2] Ibid., p. 288.
[3] Ibid., p. 278.

science. For it is not that "God" is a myth, but that myth is the revelation of a divine life in man. It is not we who invent myth, rather it speaks to us as a Word of God."[1]

The symbol or archetype of God is supreme. Jung was most careful to say that Science itself cannot determine whether the symbol is only a symbol or whether it corresponds to reality. This applies to the projection, which may both reveal our inner objects and external reality. The father or mother images are both good and bad, and the good image may be projected and appear as the good God, whilst the bad image is seen as the Devil. This is a process, and as such it cannot tell us whether God and Devil are external reality.

When the objective image of God draws into it the values of the past it becomes an image with which we can identify ourselves, 'we dwell in him, and he in us,' to our great benefit. This process may be seen as a psychological mechanism, or as bringing us into a closer relation with the living God. Psychology can show us the mechanism, but it cannot pronounce upon the living God. In passing we have mentioned the importance of the past, and we regret the suggestion has been made that we can satisfactorily forget it. We can no more live as though the past did not exist, than we can live without the future. Both past and future determine the here and now.

God is the archetype of Being at its fullest and richest, and as such it is indispensable to man. Thus when man denies God he denies himself. The result is the exaltation of himself in the place of the rejected God, and the fate of Icarus awaits him, or in Biblical imagery the confusion of Babel descends, and he loses the Paradise of which he has taken possession. The rejection of the ideal, the transcendent, leads to the primitive within himself taking possession, and against this man is powerless. The strength of the primitive lies in its great animal ancestry over which the rationality of our culture holds but the slenderest control. The humanist appeal, besides speaking to a few noble souls, addresses itself to the weakest aspect of man, the intellect, and the theologian can easily make the same mistake.

When we are admonished to look within ourselves for our salvation we are being placed in a precarious position. Although the Spirit is imminent and there is much good deep within our personality, yet there is to be found there horror unspeakable and the lawlessness of the jungle. The unconscious, as Fr Ingham has pointed out, is not to be equated with God, and Fr Victor White was right in his titling of his book *God and the Unconscious*. We shall return later to this trend which surrenders to the unconscious. The Bishop of Wool-

[1] Ibid., p. 313.

wich does not go so far as this equation, but at times he seems to be perilously near to it.

Honest to God reduces man's need of a Saviour outside himself to vanishing point, which hits hard at the traditional meaning of Christmas and Good Friday. We affirm that out of our analytical experience the concept of a supernatural intervention is often found to be of paramount importance. In Chapter 7 it was shown that when the Saviour archetype is missing the therapeutic situation is hopeless. Time after time man is at his lowest ebb, stripped of every support, of belief in himself and fellow man, whilst terrifying sinister forces claim his very soul. In such a state the patient is utterly undone, and to speak to such a man about 'the Ground of his being' makes no sense but is a diabolical mockery. Such a person's only hope is in the figure of the Saviour, someone outside and infinitely beyond himself coming to the rescue. And the wonder of it all is that the Saviour does come again and again under these conditions. The state which has been described is admittedly an extreme one, but it is in some measure very common indeed.

Jung taught us to recognize as a law of life the play of opposites. If there is dry there must also be wet; light, darkness; hot, cold. Sick people are abnormally caught up in the swing of opposites, but all of us know that we are involved in thinking and feeling in this way. It will be useless, therefore, to try to have one without the other. *Honest to God* suggests that it would be good for all of us and for the outside world in particular if we ceased to think of God as 'out there', beyond and above, and to think of Him as within, in depth. But our mental processes will not permit us to think of God in depth without thinking of Him in height, of His being within apart from His being without. Immanence implies transcendence. However, the Bishop does not dispense with the idea of transcendence, but he makes it a transcendence with the bounds of immanence. The mind will not rest in a dimension of depth unless it is balanced by what is truly high and lifted up.

This need for height as the counterpart of depth permeates our everyday thought. There is higher education, higher mathematics, we are high or low in the class, and if we are in the middle we keep an eye on either extreme. There is height in achievement or fame, or we may sink low. There are high notes and low notes, and music may sink to the lowest ebb. We may become high in our own estimation just as others are low in theirs. We may indulge in the heights of fantasy and then come down to earth, or perhaps we have to be brought down. The market has its upward and downward trends. Our reading may be high-brow or low-brow, and so on. This concern with height and depth is as deeply fixed as the hills and valleys upon which man has always gazed. The hills, as the Psalmist knew, are symbols of the eternal God above, just as the ancient Greeks, and man's much earlier ancestors, placed the abode of the Gods on the heights. Similarly the depths have been the abode of the Evil Ones. In all this there is association with light and darkness, the easy way down and the difficult ascent, 'Facilis descendus Averno' (Aen VI 126). Very often in an analysis the hill represents Calvary hill and the hard demands it places upon us. This imagery is bound with the Christmas theme of the height meeting the lowly, and out of this meeting a new Man is born.

Jung in his last work wrote:

'Who spoke to me then? Who talked of problems far beyond my knowledge? Who brought the Above and the Below together, and laid the foundation for everything that was to fill the second half of my life with stormiest passion? Who but that alien guest who came both from above and below?'[1]

'I could not yet see that interaction of both worlds which I now understand. I saw only an irreconcilable contradiction between "inner" and "outer".'[2]

And speaking of Freud he wrote:

'He was blind towards the paradox and ambiguity of the contents of the unconscious, and did not know that everything which arises out of the unconscious has a top and bottom, an inside and an outside.'[3]

A further importance of the opposites is found to be in their meeting point. This is always the point of great tension, and a position hard to deal with, for there is always the temptation to evade the issue by surrendering to one of the two extremes. The growing point in life is just where the two opposites meet. The great importance of these opposites in the deep operational base of life is something which cannot be swept aside. This is particularly true in the case of the Twice-born. To those who know the intensity of the conflict the outlook of the Once-born appears to be a gross over-simplification of life.

These criticisms of *Honest to God* are not meant to detract from other aspects of the book with which one heartily agrees and welcomes. I know from some of my patients how much they have been helped by the book.

[1] Ibid., p. 28.
[2] Ibid., p. 186.
[3] Ibid., p. 149.
The reader is referred to Jung's *Psychology and Religion*, para. 553 ff.

H

It is time to turn to the various writings of the Dean of Trinity College, Cambridge—The Reverend H. A. Williams. The Dean has very rightly seen the relevance of psychotherapy to theology, and he has made a contribution to our understanding of the impact of these two disciplines in his essay in *Soundings*. In his lecture published in *Objections to Christian Belief* he has shown to a wide public how that religion of a certain kind can blind a person to his true state. He is campaigning for reality, and with such psychotherapy is wholly concerned. All this is highly commendable. However, there are certain radical criticisms of his psychological position which we feel impelled to make.

The Once-born are not particularly troubled about their sins because they are at peace within themselves as we have already pointed out. The non-religious Once-born person never gives a thought to his sin, and accordingly he assumes he has no need for religion. Many religious Once-born people are worried because they are *not* worried about their sins, they feel there must be something wrong about their spiritual state in that they are not 'miserable sinners'. The Dean brings considerable relief to such people by showing them to be quite right in their religious attitude. On the other hand he brings nothing but confusion and distress to the Twice-born, for whom sin is the dominant reality of their lives. He fails them badly, and so would the Church were she not deeply concerned with sin. He criticizes Cranmer because there is much about sin in the Prayer Book, but it is just this which speaks to the condition of so many people. He criticizes hymns such as 'Just as I am, without one plea . . .' whereas they are magnificent instruments of the Church in dealing with the deadly guilt which harasses the lives of so many people. This hymn in particular is a first-class therapeutic exercise. The Atonement, as we usually conceive it, seems to have no part to play in meeting the burden of guilt. There is a whole dimension of human woe which seems to remain unrecognized in his writing, and this is itself a sin against the realism which the Dean so stoutly defends. Much of the therapeutic work is concerned with guilt, and this guilt is a part of reality for very many people.

The Dean's problem is one of polarity. In spite of much good in what he says on the one hand the opposite is ignored, and he repeatedly delivers himself into an extreme and one-sided position. This is dangerous, and one is impelled to say so, especially when one-sidedness is given great advertisement. One of the pitfalls of the Counsellor in therapy is that realizing how much morbid guilt and falsity has been derived from infancy to conclude that all guilt and evasion is pathological.

It is safe to assume that doctrines which have been maintained for centuries have not persisted through mere human perversity and slavery to convention. They have come down to us because they meet deep human needs. All the ding-dong of the theological discussion and statement is concerned with legitimate poles of religious experience, and we shall be very unwise to jettison doctrines just because they seem to have no relevance to our personal religious climate. There is a theology for the Once-born, and another for the Twice-born, yet these two are embraced in the width of Christian doctrine. Psychotherapy relates religion to every conceivable sort and condition of man and sees each man valuing his religion according to his life situation. No single framework or systematic presentation of Christianity is adequate. In a similar way the psychotherapist, if he is to be of the widest use to his patients, must now be of Freud, now of Jung, and now of Adler. He must resist every temptation to fit people into patterns, for in the end there will be found to be as many patterns as there are people. There is a danger that the discovery of psychology to be a handmaid unto the Lord may lead some people to adopt one-sided positions because their psychology is partial.

Another example of the extreme position of the Dean is seen in his attitude towards authority. We have noted in the previous chapters how that authority can have most damaging effects upon the personality, and the Dean is right in any criticism he may make of its misuse. However, he seems to ride too lightly over authority and tradition. There has to be authority, as I have shown, and part of the system of authority is the framework of a defined moral order. This is both for our private well-being and also for the good of society. Circumstances alter cases, but over-all it must stand or else bewilderment and confusion follow, with a resultant state of insecurity. Confusion is particularly damaging to the child, and he needs to have about him a solid framework for behaviour. The Dean is altogether right in stressing the principle of love as the ultimate guide in action, but in practice the loving course of action is often extremely difficult to assess since it involves so many issues. The best we can follow on so many occasions is a rule of thumb, and this in spite of its limitations. A wholesale rejection of normal standards is far too violent an exercise for most people. The process of change, when we are wise, takes place slowly and at the person's own pace. The person must discover for himself the new way of life, and this is usually a very long and painful process. Violent reactions can have regrettable consequences. The Dean condones ruthlessness. If it is right to be ruthless to ourselves we should be most careful in our exercise of it upon others.

Before we consider the most serious instances of onesidedness, we want to refer again to the necessity of living in the tension of opposites. We have already said that the growing point in life is the meeting of the opposite poles. God and the world, light and darkness, good and evil are of themselves extremes, and unless these meet the personality is split. Thus the growing personality must be aware of the tension and live at the point where it hurts the most. The angel and Jacob must wrestle until the light of a new day dawns. The religious language of warfare is based upon this fierce necessity. Our new theologians ignore the necessity for the conflict, and it may be because they are Once-born. This may be their besetting sin, an evasion of the pain of life, for even if we are Once-born we cannot altogether escape the tension of the opposites. This may be the reason for our feeling the new theology to be flat and unrealistic.

All of us have our dark side, 'the shadow' Jung called it. It is our private store of skeletons which we prefer to keep in the dark. Jung showed that wholeness is achieved when we recognize the shadow and come to terms with it. The dissociated part needs to be re-integrated. It is our fear of the shadow that puts most of us on our defensive, and we find ourselves doing anything rather than be confronted by it. It is naturally concerned with the animal side, with what Freud called the 'Id'. The Dean is very rightly concerned with the necessity of opening the cupboard and the bringing out into the light of day of the skeletons, but in so doing he appears to be falling into the error of embracing the opposite. He is falling over backwards in his escape from evasions and subterfuges, and thus he comes to be embraced by the Id. This is obviously no solution, although its simplicity makes it most attractive. In so doing he evades the tension of the opposites.

The Dean applauds the way in which people discover their reality, and reality is all too often for him the shadow side. The shadow remains unconfronted by the conscious self informed by well-tried disciplines and ideals. This is demonstrated in the dream described in his lecture in *Objections to Christian Belief* where a man is sitting in a theatre and seeing performers on the stage being hypnotized by a monstrous figure behind him. It was nothing less than tragic that the dreamer interpreted the dream superficially. How often people are distressed by literal interpretations of their dreams! If the dream in question had been rightly interpreted a tragedy would have been averted. Unfortunately we are not told what the people on the stage were doing, which would have given an important clue to the interpretation of the dream. The setting is a theatre, which usually in dreams is concerned with acting, i.e. unreality. The dreamer discovers a hypnotizing power at work, and the all important thing is that the power is coming from behind him, in other words it is his shadow which is causing him to be hypnotized, and also probably to perform the particular acts on the stage. This man was obviously obsessed sexually, and the poor Ego set between the shadow and the false show was completely overpowered by the two opposites. The stagey part of himself was his flight from coming to terms with his shadow. He was sitting on a volcano, the volcano of his untamed instinctual self. The eruption took place when he identified himself with his shadow, forsook his former God, and made the monstrous figure his God. This is the Great Apostasy. This was 'the beast' that rose up out of the sea (the unconscious) in Revelation XIII. This always comes about when anyone refuses to face the tensions of the opposing forces in the soul. The only way is to have courage to face the monster within ourselves, to wait upon God and the Reconciling Symbol which appears seemingly, like Melchisedec 'who saves from death,' without origin, to save. This identification with the shadow always comes about through psychological impotence. Thus the dreamer surrendered to the Evil One and turned his back upon Christ, he chose darkness rather than light. The tragedy is that he was not helped to see all this by having the help of a Christian psychotherapist.

The attitude of these writers is far too close to subjectivism to be healthy. Existentialist subjectivism and 'humanism' find the only reality to be within experience. Ideals and ideas which do not conform to this subjective reality are scorned and rejected. Albert Jung has recently reminded us[1] that such subjectivism easily swings into nihilism, with its attendant depression and despair. The reason he gives for this is that the subjective foundations cannot uphold life because they are too biological, rational and self-contained. Man's inflation cannot be sustained, and then he finds that nothing remains. In contrast with this is religion which provides a foundation for life which is other than in man himself. This foundation though discovered within experience is that 'of the eternal city' in the Heavens. Fr Victor White, in his excellent book *Soul and Psyche* showed us that our faith is no projection of the unconscious but rather a conscious seeking for and reaching out to the Beyond which responds to this seeking. The stability and meaning of a genuine religious faith meet a deep human need which nothing else can supply. And although in the course of an analysis the Christian therapist will studiously avoid any imposition of his views, he can help his patients

[1] *Analytical Psychology*, ed. Gerhard Adler.

who may seek from him a confirmation of their faith. Therapeutically this is of great value.

The findings of psychotherapy can make a most valuable contribution to theology both to purify and enrich, to affirm and to correct. But every care must be taken to ensure that the findings are well-founded, lest they be blind guides leading astray.

Any theology which gives no place to tension and conflict in life must be inadequate. The Cross will always remain the greatest of all Reconciling Symbols. Further, any theology which does not deal with guilt must be suspect.

Theology is an intellectual formulation of religion and as such it has great importance, but it must be remembered that it is incapable of giving expression to certain aspects of the personality involved in religious experience. Intuition and feeling are outside its scope. The irrational embraces many of the greatest values, for example, love. God is love. The deepest experiences can only be expressed by symbol and myth. To know is therefore to experience, to live through. The reach of the symbol is wider than the individual's experience, it embraces the Collective. Thus it involves us in mystery. Theology, like all the sciences, must realize its limitations.

THE CHURCH AND CHILD GUIDANCE[1]

The Church offers to God the work and service of man. The 'cup of cold water' given in His Name is service done to Him. The world at large has some inkling of this when it professes that 'deeds speak louder than words.' Whether we like it or not the world measures our sincerity by our usefulness to our fellow-man. We therefore bring honour and glory to God by showing to the world that we mean business in practical affairs. A travesty of the Christian Way is presented when we merely protest against modern trends, and demand that the course of change be stopped and that a former pattern be restored. No wonder that we are just passed by when we try to do this. Further, to be seen to be playing with life superficially not only achieves nothing but is definitely off-putting, and endorses the idea that the Church is completely irrelevant to modern society.

The real issues which harass people are not resolved by stock-in-trade answers, but each of them demands an individual treatment, and often a treatment which is outside the scope of a purely rational resolution. In order to be found in touch with life where it pinches most we must exercise a ministry at the very centre of human relatedness, bringing sympathetic care and penetrating understanding at every point. Because we have failed to do this we have both lost ground and lost face, and an effort here is being made to show how the years which the locusts have eaten may be restored.

The Mothers' Union and the Young Wives' Fellowship satisfy an important need of the Church in that they provide fellowship. What is about to be said is by no means suggesting that social activities should be cut out of their programmes. There are times when it is right to have evening outings, and a talk on the relative merits of gas and electric cookers. But what an opportunity is lost when little more than this is achieved. The main concern of these parts of the Church must be the serious business of life with special reference to the problems and relationships of the home. Such problems are obviously more the concern of the Young Wives' Fellowship, but the experience of the members of the Mothers' Union may be found to

[1] A suggestion submitted for consideration to the authorities at Mary Sumner House.

be helpful to the younger mothers, and the older generation in some cases will be found in need of considerable education.

Everything which is the concern of the mother should be the concern of the Young Wives' Fellowship, and these concerns are mainly related to her babies and their growing up, her husband and her home. The many problems which arise cannot be left to Nature to resolve for the very reason that we are not living 'according to nature'. Life is far removed from the simple life of the individual in the primitive community. Both the parent and the child are subjected to unnatural pressures which cannot be avoided, such as the competitiveness and rivalry which our educational system creates, the stress of living in an atomic age, the pressures by countless distractions and interests, the problem of sex which unnatural advertising of the subject in television, magazine, novel and theatre accentuates. Everyday life becomes more difficult to manage, and therefore, those most directly responsible for giving help to the young should be themselves offered help by the Church, the Mother of us all.

The Christian home is often spoken of as a standard kind home, whereas there are as many varieties of the Christian home as there are varieties of people who comprise the homes. In the Christian home there are however certain attitudes in common regarding the significance of human existence, the sources of refreshment of the human spirit, and certain 'values'. Yet there may lurk a hidden and destructive thing in the very bosom of the Christian home, and of this we need to be fully aware, for when we are blind to it, as this book has shown, it can easily stultify the total effort for the well-being of the family. The splendid aspects of the Christian home can be so emphasized that the value of the individual members of the family is not established. The unity of the home is given priority with the result that parents and children are submerged by their own totalitarianism. The home has great value, but it is value for the development of each member of the home, and this ceases as soon as the home itself becomes dominant. The home has value only so long as there is encouragement of, and respect for, individual differences. There must be a give and take, and a constant learning from one another. It is fatal to allow the giving of advice to be all on the one side, and the reception to be equally onesided. There must be held a balanced love for neighbour and love of oneself, a respect for one's own views and a respect for those of others. These must never be allowed to become an 'either or', in which case we surrender our own value or become egotistical and anti-social. In order to become a whole person each member of the family must be allowed a place for *his* own individuality, and he must respect that of the other members of the family. The Self and the Other must be kept in balance. This is anything but easy to achieve, yet apart from it all our labour to make a Christian home may be lost. This is an instance of how all the goodwill in the world can go hopelessly wrong unless it is allied to an understanding of human need.

The gangster was once a child, he was a baby, subjected to various influences in the home. He might have become a 'saint'. Our children are being turned one way or the other, and in ways which cannot be corrected, humanly speaking, apart from an understanding of life from the child's point of view. The great tragedy of the past is that we have not been aware of what we have been doing to our children. We may endeavour now to correct this in our dealings with our own children. We can learn what it is which makes a child over-dependent and clinging, or what makes him excessively self-sufficient. In the past we have been content to say they were born different, but now we know otherwise. Of course, there are temperamental differences, but these are easily exaggerated, whilst the harmful formations caused by parental mishandling have been overlooked. All this has a direct bearing upon the reason why some children do not 'take to religion'. Thus the Church should offer all possible help to parents and to our young mothers in particular upon whose shoulders so much of the burden must lie.

It will be a great day for the Church when it becomes known that the Young Wives' Fellowship comes to be valued as a counselling service for the upbringing of children in the best possible way. When the Outsider learns from her neighbour that child problems are discussed and help is given in the Young Wives' Fellowship it may not only save children from growing up into people whose lives are distorted and a misery to themselves and others, but also a new appreciation of the Church will be the gain. Knowing people as we do it may well be that we should lose some members of our organization because they are afraid of facing life problems within themselves, and prefer to live in their own private cuckoo-land of ignorance. But at least they will know in their hearts that they have run away. The majority of people, who mean business in the bringing up of their families, would welcome the Church's help and be all the more confirmed in their membership.

What is called for is new concern with life's problems. First, such problems as those which the baby has to meet, and here much will be learned about the great importance of the right feeding of the infant, toilet-training (concerning which there is the greatest mishandling of the infant), and kindred subjects, all of which have the utmost effect upon the subsequent life of the person. The many problems of the young child will be dealt with; why, for example, he is obstinate, showing off, shy, or why he has the tantrums or the sulks. These, and many more such like characteristics in the child are but symptoms of vital problems which must be solved if the child is to grow up giving full service to God and man, a happy person in himself and good to live with. There is need to understand life from the eldest child's point of view, and from the youngest's, or from that of the middle child.

As the child grows up sex comes into the picture, and there is help needed in coping with this situation. There are educational problems relating to the backward or deficient child, or the pressure of school work and the over-emphasis upon the intellect. Later still, are the adolescent concern, and vocation, youth and the Church.

Passing from these we come to the problems of early marriage, middle-age marriage, divorce, prostitution, and other moral irresponsibilities. There is far more behind the scenes than meets the eye on these important subjects, and we should know a vast amount about them. If we are to do our job as Christians we must do something other than shake our heads and say we 'don't know what things are coming to.' Such grandmotherly attitudes do not become a Church. It may hurt us to delve into the deep springs of life, but who said we should not be hurt as we go out to seek and to save those who are lost in the entanglements of life? If we meet the issues of modern living, or even make an attempt to meet them, we shall gain the respect of the world, which may well be the first step towards winning the world for our Lord.

The primary object must be to give people a new standpoint; to open eyes which have been closed, and to open ears which have not before heard such things. How is this to be achieved? I suggest by means of discussion groups. It does not matter all that much what kind of conclusions are reached, at first at any rate, the chief thing is to see into a new and unsuspected level of life which controls much of life's activity and quality. To help the Young Wives' Fellowship in this I suggest that a series of pamphlets be produced, written with group-discussion in mind, on many subjects, including the few I have mentioned above. Not too difficult books could be circulated for further reading. These pamphlets should be written by the best authorities on the various subjects. For the discussion there should be permanent small groups. It might be possible to obtain qualified speakers on special subjects, although it is obvious that we should have to rely mainly on self-help. When the Church has a trained Ministry in Counselling much more help will be available.

I return to the question: Are we going to allow the world to pass us by as incompetent to deal with life and as an obsolete irrelevance? Are we content to see our children, the children of the Church, caught up in the vast neurosis of our time and suffer beyond measure through our criminal neglect of vital care and understanding? I hope the Church through the vast potential of the Mothers' Union and Young Wives' Fellowship will be brave enough to prove to the world her worth in this most practical way, and play a decisive part in shaping a new age by taking into herself this singular service.

GENERAL INDEX

INDEX OF SCRIPTURE REFERENCES

GEORGE ALLEN & UNWIN LTD

London: 40 Museum Street, WC1

Auckland: 24 Wyndham Street
Bombay: 15 Graham Road, Ballard Estate, Bombay 1
Bridgetown: P.O. Box 222
Buenos Aires: Escritorio 454–459, Florida 165
Calcutta: 17 Chittaranjan Avenue, Calcutta 13
Cape Town: 109 Long Street
Hong Kong: 44 Mody Road, Kowloon
Ibadan: P.O. Box 62
Karachi: Karachi Chambers, McLeod Road
Madras: Mohan Mansions, 38c Mount Road, Madras 6
Mexico: Villalongin 32–10, Piso, Mexico 5, D.F.
Nairobi: P.O. Box 4536
New Delhi: 13–14 Asaf Ali Road, New Delhi 1
Sao Paulo: Avenida 9 De Julho 1138–Ap. 51
Singapore: 36c Princep Street, Singapore 7
Sydney: N.S.W.: Bradbury House, 55 York Street
Tokyo: 10 Kanda-Ogawamachi, 3-Chome, Chiyoda-Ku
Toronto: 91 Wellington Street West, Toronto 1

FREUD: A CRITICAL RE-EVALUATION

In this book Dr Fine sets out to describe what Freud said, and to re-evaluate his views critically in the light of the best knowledge today.

Freud's numerous changes of view, his constant searching for the truth wherever it might lead him, as well as his resolute adherence to certain hard-won positions once he had achieved them, are all skilfully traced. Freud's intellectual Odyssey is divided into four periods. From 1886 to 1895 he was a neurologist investigating hysteria and other 'nervous' disorders. Then came this self-analysis, from 1896 to 1899, the real matrix from which psychoanalysis grew. The first psycho-analytic system of psychology was developed in the period from 1900 to 1914. The remainder of his life, from 1914 to 1939, was devoted to the elaboration of ego psychology, and heart of contemporary psycho-analysis.

Dr Fine undertook, in writing this book, the formidable task of examining the whole body of Freud's thought, to clarify what he said, and to review his ideas critically in the light of the best available existing knowledge. As he says 'In this process of criticism I have tried to specify which aspects of Freud have stood the test of time and which have not.

'So far as I can see no one has ever before taken the trouble to ask: "What did Freud actually say? How does what Freud said stand up in terms of what we now know?"'

In answering these questions, Dr Fine develops a major thesis that all modern psycho-analysis derives from Freud, though it has moved far in many different directions. The contention is that emphasis on schools is misleading and has obscured the actual historical growth of the science.

As he states in his Preface to this volume, Dr Fine's conviction is: 'By building on Freud's fundamental insights, we can move on most readily to empirical research and thus construct a more satisfactory science of psychology.'

'Dr Fine does an admirable job of clarification and exposition. His book should hereafter prove invaluable to all students of Freud who want a short cut to mastering the tortuous unwindings of his complex theories.'—*Dr Richard Peters* in *Nation*.
Demy 8vo.
                                                        35s. net

GEORGE ALLEN AND UNWIN LTD

In his new book, Canon Ducker makes a f
attempt to convince the Church of the
opportunity which the application of p.
therapy provides, both to enrich her o
and to demonstrate the relevance of her i
...ychotherapy reveals our hidden d...